INIQUITY TRAP

Copyright 2023

All rights reserved. No part of this publication may be reproduced without the prior permission of the publisher.

This book is protected by United States copyright laws.

Scripture reference in this book are taken from THE HOLY BIBLE, NEW INTERNATIONAL VERSION®, NIV® Copyright © 1973, 1978, 1984, 2011 by Biblica, Inc. ™ Used by permission. All rights reserved worldwide.

Scripture quotations taken from the New American Standard Bible® marked (NASB), Copyright © 1960, 1962, 1963, 1968, 1971, 1972, 1973, 1975, 1977, 1995 by The Lockman Foundation Used by permission. (www. Lockman.org) Scripture quotations marked "KJV" are taken from the Holy Bible, King James Version, Cambridge, 1769.

Scripture quotations marked (NLT) are taken from the Holy Bible, New Living Translation, copyright © 1996, 2004, 2007 by Tyndale House Foundation. Used by permission of Tyndale House Publishers, Inc., Carol Stream, Illinois 60188. All rights reserved.

The Living Bible copyright © 1971 by Tyndale House Foundation. Used by permission of Tyndale House Publishers Inc., Carol Stream, Illinois, 60188. All rights reserved.

Scripture texts in this work are taken from the New American Bible, revised edition © 2010, 1991, 1986, 1970 Confraternity of Christian Doctrine, Washington, D.C. and are used by permission of the copyright owner. All Rights Reserved.

Scriptures marked ISV are taken from the INTERNATIONAL STANDARD VERSION (ISV): Scripture taken from INTERNATIONAL STANDARD VERSION, copyright©1996-2008 by the ISV Foundation. All rights reserved internationally.

Scriptures marked TM are taken from the THE MESSAGE: THE BIBLE IN CONTEMPORARY ENGLISH (TM): copyright©1993, 1994, 1995, 1996, 2000, 2001, 2002. Used by permission of NavPress Publishing Group.

"Scripture quotations taken from the Amplified® Bible, Copyright © 1954, 1958, 1962,1964, 1965, 1987 by the Lockman Foundation Used by permission. (www.Lockman.org).

The Message is quoted: "Scripture taken from The Message. Copyright © 1993, 1995, 1996, 2000, 2001, 2002. Used by permission of NavPress Publishing Group."

"Scripture quotations are from the ESV® Bible (The Holy Bible, English Standard Version®), copyright © 2001 by Crossway, a publishing ministry of Good News Publishers. Used by permission. All rights reserved."

Scripture quoted by permission. Quotations designated (NET) are from the NET Bible® copyright ©1996-2016 by Biblical Studies Press, LLC.http://netbible.org All rights reserved.

The Hebrew Names Version is based off the World English Bible, an update of the American Standard Version of 1901. This version of the Bible is in the public domain,

V Ly Publishing LLC
8758 Dunn LN E.
Olive Branch, MS 38654

ISBN: 978-1-942484-03-5

Iniquity Trap

Contents

Introduction 1

Chapter 1: Iniquity 3

Chapter 2: Origins Of Iniquity 5

Chapter 3: Iniquity Transfers 7

Chapter 4: Adam's Family Iniquity 9

Chapter 5: Fathers - An Accounting System 13

Chapter 6: Why Iniquity Transfers 15

Chapter 7: Guilt's Flow 17

Chapter 8: Guilt Train 19

Chapter 9: Enticed To Sin 21

Chapter 10: Repetition in Iniquity 23

Chapter 11: King David's Iniquity 25

Chapter 12: Brother by Another Mother? 27

Chapter 13: Iniquity in David's Family 31

Chapter 14: Victims of Iniquity 35

Chapter 15: The Visit 37

Chapter 16: Adopted Children and Iniquity 39

Chapter 17: When a Generation Dies 41

Chapter 18: Iniquity of Scribes and Pharisees 43

Chapter 19: Jesus Defeats Iniquity 45

Chapter 20: Jesus the Redeemer 47

Chapter 21: Blood and Atonement 49

Chapter 22: The Blood of Jesus 51

Chapter 23: Authority of the Name of Jesus 53

Chapter 24: Nephilim in the Blood Line 55

Chapter 25: Judgement on Earth 57

Chapter 26: Genealogy of Heaven or Earth 61

Chapter 27: Who's Your Daddy? 63

Iniquity Trap Workbook 65

- Iniquity Chart 67
- Iniquity Trap Chart 157
- Prayer to Remove Iniquity 179
  - Prayer to Forgive Anger. 179
  - Prayer to Forgive. 179
  - Prayers for Iniquity. 179
  - Prayer to Remove a Specific Iniquity. 179
  - Prayer to Remove all Iniquity, Sin, and Guilt. 179
  - Prayer to Remove Any Physical or Mental Illness. 180
  - Prayer for Victims of Abuse 180
  - Prayer to Receive Family Blessings. 180
- Scripture References on Sin 181
  - Lust of the Flesh Scripture 181
  - Lust of the Eyes 182
  - Pride of Life 182
  - Ten Commandments 182

Introduction

Iniquity can move in a family line without much resistance. Understanding and recognizing how it works proves to be eye opening. Once observed in your own life, an iniquity cycle can be stopped. With this information, the next generation will know what to guard against. In reading this book, along with completing the worksheets, I pray the Lord will open your eyes and understanding to the iniquity trap.

Chapter 1
Iniquity

To gain understanding of iniquity we must turn to the Bible. Moses was called to lead Israel to their promise land. This proved to be a difficult task as God's people repeatedly grumbled and rebelled. So, one day Moses made a request of the Lord. "If I have found favor in your sight, please show me now your ways, that I may know you in order to find favor in your sight. Consider too that this nation is your people." (Exodus 33:13 ESV) Moses said, "Please show me your glory." (Exodus 33:18)

Moses sought the Presence of the Lord to go with them and to know God's ways. From the Lord's answer, we discover God's heart and the generational problem of iniquity (Exodus 33:12-23).

> So, "the LORD passed by before him, and proclaimed, The LORD, The LORD God, merciful and gracious, longsuffering, and abundant in goodness and truth, keeping mercy for thousands, forgiving iniquity and transgression and sin, and that will not clear the guilty; visiting the iniquity of the fathers upon the children, and upon the children's children, unto the third and to the fourth generation." (Exodus 34:7 KJB)

In this scripture God reveals the abundance of his goodness and mercy. We also discover that he forgives iniquity, transgression, and sin. Let's find out the distinction between these terms. Iniquity avon (Strong #H5771) means perversity, i.e. (moral) evil: —fault, mischief, punishment (of iniquity);[1] The root word for avon means to bend, twist, distort.[2]

In considering iniquity one needs to look at the root word for perversity. Perverse means "willfully determined or disposed to go counter to what is expected or desired; contrary. Turning away from what is right; rejecting what was right. And persistent in what is wrong."[3]

Using iniquity's Hebrew root word avah (Strong's H5753), perversity draws a person to bend, twist, or distort a command of God. God set the standard and turning from his word demonstrates perversity. Transgression, Hebrew pesha (Strong's H6588), describes "a revolt: rebellion, sin."[4]

Sin is "an offense and its penalty: to miss or err from the mark."[5] The progression comes by tempting a person to willfully revolt from the word of God and then sin.

The International Standard Bible Encyclopedia provides an overview of iniquity from the Bible.

> In the Old Testament of the 11 words translated "iniquity," by far the most common and important is (Strong #H5771) avon (awon, (ʻāôn) (about 215 times). Etymologically, it is customary to explain it as meaning literally "crookedness," "perverseness," i.e., evil regarded as that which is not straight or upright, moral distortion (from ʻiwwah, "to bend," "make crooked," "pervert"). In actual usage it has three meanings which almost imperceptibly pass into each other:

3

(1) iniquity,

(2) guilt of iniquity,

(3) punishment of iniquity.

Primarily, it denotes "not an action, but the character of an action" (Oehler) and is so distinguished from "sin" (chatta'th). Hence, we have the expression "the iniquity of my sin" (Psalms 32:5). Thus the meaning glides into that of "guilt," which might often take the place of "iniquity" as the translation of `awon (Genesis 15:16; Exodus 34:7; Jeremiah 2:22, etc.). From "guilt" it again passes into the meaning of "punishment of guilt," just as Latin piaculum may denote both guilt and its punishment. The transition is all the easier in Hebrew because of the Hebrew sense of the intimate relation of sin and suffering, e.g. Genesis 4:13, "My punishment is greater than I can bear"; which is obviously to be preferred to King James Version margin, the Revised Version, margin "Mine iniquity is greater than can be forgiven," for Cain is not so much expressing sorrow for his sin, as complaining of the severity of his punishment; compare 2 Kings 7:9 (the Revised Version (British and American) "punishment," the Revised Version margin "iniquity"); Isaiah 5:18 (where for "iniquity" we might have "punishment of iniquity," as in Leviticus 26:41,43, etc.); Isaiah 40:2 ("iniquity," the Revised Version margin "punishment"). The phrase "bear iniquity" is a standing expression for bearing its consequences, i.e. its penalty; generally of the sinner bearing the results of his own iniquity (Leviticus 17:16; 20:17,19; Numbers 14:34; Ezekiel 44:10, etc.), but sometimes of one bearing the iniquity of another vicariously, and so taking it away (e.g. Ezekiel 4:4; 18:19 f). Of special interest in the latter sense are the sufferings of the Servant of Yahweh, who shall "bear the iniquities" of the people (Isaiah 53:11; compare Isaiah 53:6).

Other words frequently translated "iniquity" are:
`awen, literally, "worthlessness," "vanity," hence, "naughtiness," "mischief" (47 times in the King James Version, especially in the phrase "workers of iniquity," Job 4:8; Psalms 5:5; 6:8; Proverbs 10:29, etc.); `awel and `awlah, literally, "perverseness" (Deuteronomy 32:4; Job 6:29 the King James Version, etc.).

In the New Testament "iniquity" stands for anomia equals properly, "the condition of one without law," "lawlessness" (so translated in 1John 3:4, elsewhere "iniquity," e.g. Matthew 7:23), a word which frequently stood for `awon in the Septuagint; and adikia, literally, "unrighteousness" (e.g. Luke 13:27). D. Miall Edwards [6]

Footnotes

[1] "H5771 - `avon – Strong's Hebrew Lexicon (KJV)." Blue Letter Bible. Web. 25 Oct 2019.

[2] "H5753 - `avah – Strong's Hebrew Lexicon (KJV)." Blue Letter Bible. Web. 25 Oct 2019.

[3] "Perverse." Dictionary.com, Dictionary.com, 24 Oct. 2019,

[4] "H6588 – pesha` - Strong's Hebrew Lexicon (KJV)." Blue Letter Bible. Web. 19 Dec 2019.

[5] "H2403 – chatta'ath – Strong's Hebrew Lexicon (KJV)." Blue Letter Bible. Web. 31 Dec 2019.

[6] Edwards, D. "Iniquity - International Standard Bible Encyclopedia." Blue Letter Bible. 5 May 2003. Web. 20 Dec 2022.

Chapter 2
Origins Of Iniquity

The book of Ezekiel reveals the existence of iniquity coming first out of the spirit realm, certainly not from God, but a fallen cherub angel. The New Living Translation Bible provides a good description of this angel prior to his fall.

"…You were the model of perfection, full of wisdom and exquisite in beauty.[13] You were in Eden, the garden of God. Your clothing was adorned with every precious stone—red carnelian, pale-green peridot, white moonstone, blue-green beryl, onyx, green jasper, blue lapis lazuli, turquoise, and emerald—all beautifully crafted for you and set in the finest gold. They were given to you on the day you were created.[14] I ordained and anointed you as the mighty angelic guardian. You had access to the holy mountain of God and walked among the stones of fire. [15] "You were blameless in all you did from the day you were created until the day evil was found in you.[16] Your rich commerce led you to violence, and you sinned. So, I banished you in disgrace from the mountain of God. I expelled you, O mighty guardian, from your place among the stones of fire.[17] Your heart was filled with pride because of all your beauty. Your wisdom was corrupted by your love of splendor. Ezekiel 28:12b-17 NLT

Here also are a few quick Bible verses about this angel.

"You were in Eden, the garden of God." (Ezekiel 28:13)

"You [were] the anointed cherub who covers; I established you…" (Ezekiel 28:14a NKJV)

"You [were] perfect in your ways from the day you were created, till iniquity was found in you." (Ezekiel 28:15 KJV)

"Your heart became proud on account of your beauty, and you corrupted your wisdom because of your splendor." (Ezekiel 28:17 NIV)

"I will ascend above the tops of the clouds; I will make myself like the Most High." [Isaiah 14:14 NIV]

God described Lucifer as a perfect angel until iniquity was discovered in him. Iniquity evel (Strong's H5766) in Ezekiel 28:15 reveals "moral evil, wickedness, depravity."[1] Evel comes from the Hebrew root word aval (Strong's H5765) meaning to "turn away from, to distort, to decline especially from what is right."[2] Once holy, Lucifer's heart became proud, and his wisdom corrupt (Ezekiel 28:15-16). Lucifer revolted from the authority of God the Father who created him. He then set out to exalt himself as God (Isaiah 14:15).

Lucifer became the first being with iniquity. He perverted his way, turned away from righteousness and sinned. Through him iniquity spread and infected one-third of all angels. Every fallen angel received Satan's vile nature which came out of his iniquity. Both Satan and these angels were thrown out of heaven (Revelation 12:3; 7-9).

Next Satan transferred his iniquity to Adam and Eve in the Garden of Eden (Genesis 3:1-6). When Satan got close to Eve, the spirit of pride which Satan carried released its tempting poison: "she could be like God" (Genesis 3:5). Satan seemed to be aware of God's command to this couple. My guess is Eve told him. She did not seem to have a problem talking to him. One day the serpent approached Eve challenging the command from God. He challenged the word God originally commanded Adam (Genesis 2:16-17).

> "One day he asked the woman, "Did God really say you must not eat the fruit from any of the trees in the garden" 2 The woman said to the serpent, "We may eat fruit from the trees in the garden, 3 but God did say, 'You must not eat fruit from the tree that is in the middle of the garden, and you must not touch it, or you will die.'"4 "You will not certainly die," the serpent said to the woman. 5 "For God knows that when you eat from it your eyes will be opened, and you will be like God, knowing good and evil." 6 When the woman saw that the fruit of the tree was good for food and pleasing to the eye, and also desirable for gaining wisdom, she took some and ate it. She also gave some to her husband, who was with her, and he ate it. 7 Then the eyes of both of them were opened, and they realized they were naked; so they sewed fig leaves together and made coverings for themselves. (Genesis 3:1-7)

When Adam and Eve fell, they became guilty of sin. Satan successfully transferred the process of iniquity, sin, guilt, and death to all people.

The progression God exposed in Exodus 34:7 began with iniquity. It led to rebellion, also known as transgression. Transgression occurs after a person perverts the word of God or twists it to meet their selfish desire. Sin is the offense which takes place after a person perverts, then revolts from God's word. Iniquity originating from Satan transferred to all mankind through Adam and Eve. This same pattern of iniquity entrapment passed down to the generations.

Footnotes

[1] "H5766 - `evel - Strong's Hebrew Lexicon (KJV)." Blue Letter Bible. Web. 28 Nov 2019.

[22] "H5765 - `aval - Strong's Hebrew Lexicon (KJV)." Blue Letter Bible. Web. 28 Nov 2019.

Chapter 3
Iniquity Transfers

Originally iniquity moved from Lucifer to Adam and Eve. This opened the door for demonic oppression to waltz through our families. Understanding one's family iniquity can prove to be invaluable.

Consider the first family with an example of iniquity from Adam to Cain. Adam's sin brought death. Sometime later, "sin" approached Cain.

> 6 Then the LORD said to Cain, "Why are you angry? And why has your countenance fallen? 7 "If you do well, will not your countenance be lifted up? And if you do not do well, sin is crouching at the door; and its desire is for you, but you must master "it". (Genesis 4:6-7 NASB)

This reveals a visit by an evil spirit to the next generation. Its purpose, to tempt and transfer iniquity by sin to the next generation. Here we also discover the initial use of the word "sin" in the Bible.

Sin has desire. Sin's desire came from the iniquity passed down from Adam. Adam entered spiritual death by rebelling from God's word. In Genesis 4:7 God told Cain how to stand against iniquity. "If you do well," and not give into sin or pervert your way, then sin cannot have you (Genesis 4:7). Cain yielded to sin anyway and a devil acquired access to him. Thus, an evil spirit gained an open door to move through Cain's family line.

Here are some interesting facts about sin in Genesis 4:7. Sin is called an "it" (NASB)." The Darby Bible refers to sin here as a "he". Furthermore, sin just happens to be a noun, "meaning a crouching beast".[1] This crouching beast (an evil spirit) came to twist "death," giving it another method to end life. Adam's disobedience to God's word, released spiritual and physical death. Cain's disobedience to God's word, released death through violence by murder. Interestingly, this first murder occurred by yielding to the instigation of an evil spirit.

CHAPTER 4
ADAM'S FAMILY INIQUITY

After Adam sinned, he died at the age of 930 years old. In the second generation from Adam, death twisted and took another form other than natural death. Iniquity bearing death targeted the next generation of Adam's seed. Cain's murder of his own brother became the first murder in the Bible. Abel's murder also took the life of a member of Adam's family. Adam and Eve became the first family to grieve over a murdered child.

Additionally, Adam's sin brought death and separation from God his Father. Death likewise separated Adam from his son Abel. Then God banished Cain from living in the land. Therefore, Adam no longer had Cain around either. Thus, Adam lost both sons due to iniquity.

Since iniquity functioned in the first family in this way, pay attention. One can yield to iniquity and sin. Or become an innocent victim of the one who yielded. Iniquity can play out either way. This occurred in King David's family too.

As a consequence of sin, Cain became a nomadic, wanderer. He reaped a cursed ground that no longer produced as before (Genesis 4:14). Cain took Abel's life, so Cain lost the life he previously enjoyed.

Adam's sin brought spiritual separation from God. Cain furthermore left the Presence of God, which was an actual separation from God also. He went to the land of Nod (wandering) where his first son Enoch was born. Cain then built a walled city for protection, an indication that Cain "feared" someone would murder him, just as he did his brother (Genesis 4:11-16). Satan gained access not only to Cain, but to his descendants (Genesis 4:1-8).

> 17 Cain had relations with his wife and she conceived and gave birth to Enoch; and he built a city, and called the name of the city Enoch, after the name of his son. 18 Now to Enoch was born Irad and Irad became the father of Mehujael, and Mehujael became the father of Methushael, and Methushael became the father of Lamech. (Genesis 4:17-18 NASB)

(To set the stage for the rest of Iniquity Trap, the following is an excerpt from my book *Origins of a Psychopath*.)

Not much information is given in Scripture about the descendants of Cain, but Hebrew names and their meanings give insight. By these one may recognize sin's transference through Cain's family line (Genesis 17:5).[1]

Enoch's name is defined as "dedicated," as this first city was dedicated to Cain's son. Enoch's son Irad's name means "Fugitive or wild ass." Mehujael means "smitten by God," and Methushael, "man of God, or suppliant." Irad, a fugitive, indicates lawlessness. Mehujael, Irad's son, was struck down by God which conveys he also was an evil man. Son of Mehujael, Methushael's name, indicates he became a "man of God." In any family line, a person can reject sin and turn to God, as it seems Methushael may have done. Then consider Lamech from Cain's lineage that killed a man and a boy. Lamech furthermore became the first polygamist who took two wives.[23456]

Iniquity visits to the third and fourth generation. We will begin with Cain but do not know much about Cain's son, Enoch. But his grandson Irad was named as a fugitive. Next, his son in the fourth generation, Mehujael, was so evil God put an end to him. In the fifth generation Methushael cried out to God. Lamech, Methushael's son, commits murders and marries two women at once. Lamech was the third generation from Irad, the fugitive. Each father may have his sins repeat to the third and fourth generations, as occurred from Irad. In Cain's family line, we note lawlessness, murder, fugitives, and one so evil God struck him down. Also, from Cain's line the marriage covenant established by God became altered.

After Cain murdered Abel, God enabled Adam and Eve to conceive another son, Seth. Let us take a look at his lineage.

> 6 Seth lived one hundred and five years, and became the father of Enosh. 9 Enosh lived ninety years, and became the father of Kenan. 12 Kenan lived seventy years and became the father of Mahalalel. 13 Then Kenan lived eight hundred and forty years after he became the father of Mahalalel … and he had other sons and daughters. 15 Mahalalel lived sixty-five years, and became the father of Jared. 18 Jared lived one hundred and sixty-two years, and became the father of Enoch. 21 Enoch lived sixty-five years, and became the father of Methuselah. 23 So all the days of Enoch were three hundred and sixty-five years. 24 Enoch walked with God; and he was not, for God took him. 25 Methuselah lived one hundred and eighty-seven years, and became the father of Lamech. 28 Lamech lived one hundred and eighty-two years, and became the father of a son. 29 Now he called his name Noah, saying, "This one will give us rest from our work and from the toil of our hands arising from the ground which the LORD has cursed." 30 Then Lamech lived five hundred and ninety-five years after he became the father of Noah, and he had other sons and daughters. 32 Noah was five hundred years old, and Noah became the father of Shem, Ham, and Japheth. (Genesis 5:6, 9, 12, 13, 15, 18, 21, 25, 27, 28-30 NASB)

By definitions let's see what we can find. Seth's first son Enosh's name, means "man." Enosh's son Kenan's name means "possession." Kenan's son Mahalaleel's name means "praise of God." Mahalaleel's son Jared means, "descent." Jared had a son named Enoch, whose name indicates life and "dedicated" to God. He pleased God so much God took him to heaven without dying (Genesis 5:24). Enoch's son Methuselah's name was "man of the dart," who lived longer than any other in the Bible and after his death, the flood came. Methuselah also had a son he named Lamech, who became the father of Noah. Lamech is defined as "powerful," and Noah's name means "rest." By Noah's faith and trust in God, he demonstrated the way to find "rest." Noah believed God's Word, which saved him and his family from destruction.[78910111213]

Both Cain and Seth had the same parents but turned out so differently. Cain and Seth made drastically different choices for their lives. Cain did not resist evil, so evil overcame him, and then evil moved through his descendants. Seth chose righteousness, and his descendants walked in the blessing of his decision.

Ezekiel 28 gives an overview of how each person can decide whether he or she will follow in the ways of the previous generation.

4"Behold, all souls are Mine; the soul of the father as well as the soul of the son is Mine. The soul who sins will die. 5"But if a man is righteous and practices justice and righteousness, 6and does not eat at the mountain [shrines] or lift up his eyes to the idols of the house of Israel, or defile his neighbor's wife or approach a woman during her menstrual period-- 7if a man does not oppress anyone, but restores to the debtor his pledge, does not commit robbery, [but] gives his bread to the hungry and covers the naked with clothing, 8if he does not lend [money] on interest or take increase, [if] he keeps his hand from iniquity [and] executes true~ justice between man and man, 9[if] he walks in My statutes and My ordinances so as to deal faithfully-- he is righteous [and] will surely live," declares the Lord GOD. 10"Then he may have a violent son who sheds blood and who does any of these things to a brother 11(though he himself did not do any of these things), that is, he even eats at the mountain [shrines], and defiles his neighbor's wife, 12oppresses the poor and needy, commits robbery, does not restore a pledge, but lifts up his eyes to the idols [and] commits abomination, 13he lends [money] on interest and takes increase; will he live? He will not live! He has committed all these abominations, he will surely be put to death; his blood will be on his own head. 14"Now behold, he has a son who has observed all his father's sins which he committed, and observing does not do likewise. 15"He does not eat at the mountain [shrines] or lift up his eyes to the idols of the house of Israel, or defile his neighbor's wife, 16or oppress anyone, or retain a pledge, or commit robbery, [but] he gives his bread to the hungry and covers the naked with clothing, 17he keeps his hand from the poor, does not take interest or increase, [but] executes My ordinances, and walks in My statutes; he will not die for his father's iniquity, he will surely live. 18"As for his father, because he practiced extortion, robbed [his] brother and did what was not good among his people, behold, he will die for his iniquity. (Ezekiel 18:4-18 NASB)

Footnotes

[1] Klein, John, and Adam Spears. Devils and Demons and the Return of the Nephilim. Fairfax: Xulon Press, 2005. P.82. May 7, 2012.

[2] Blue Letter Bible. "Dictionary and Word Search for Chanowk (Strong's 2585)". Blue Letter Bible. 1996-2011.

[3] Blue Letter Bible. "Dictionary and Word Search for `Iyrad (Strong's 5897)". Blue Letter Bible. 1996-2011.

[4] Blue Letter Bible. "Dictionary and Word Search for Měchuwya'el (Stro ng's 4232)". Blue Letter Bible. 1996-2011.

[5] Blue Letter Bible. "Dictionary and Word Search for Měthuwsha'el (Strong's 4967)". Blue Letter Bible. 1996-2011.

[6] Blue Letter Bible. "Dictionary and Word Search for Lemek (Strong's 3929)". Blue Letter Bible. 1996-2011.

[7] Blue Letter Bible. "Dictionary and Word Search for 'Enowsh (Strong's 583)". Blue Letter Bible. 1996-2011.

[8] Blue Letter Bible. "Dictionary and Word Search for Qeynan (Strong's 7018)". Blue Letter Bible. 1996-2011.

[9] Blue Letter Bible. "Dictionary and Word Search for Mahalal'el (Strong's 4111)". Blue Letter Bible. 1996-2011.

[10] Blue Letter Bible. "Dictionary and Word Search for Yered (Strong's 3382)". Blue Letter Bible. 1996-2011.

[11] Blue Letter Bible. "Dictionary and Word Search for Chanowk (Strong's 2585)". Blue Letter Bible. 1996-2011.

[12] Blue Letter Bible. "Dictionary and Word Search for Lemek (Strong's 3929)". Blue Letter Bible. 1996-2011.

[13] Blue Letter Bible. "Dictionary and Word Search for Noach (Strong's 5146)". Blue Letter Bible. 1996-2011. https://www.gotquestions.org/Does the Bible mention David's mother?.html.

Chapter 5
Fathers – An Accounting System

We know sin is simply a "transgression of God's known will or any principle or law."[1] Sin transfers from one generation to the next through the iniquity of the fathers onto their children to the third and fourth generations (Exodus 20:5, 7, Deuteronomy 5:9-10).[2] Another term for this is generational sin because a particular sin or transgression can be found from generation to generation in a family's bloodline. Some might think, "Wait a minute. What about mothers?" We see transferable sin from mothers, but a father is accountable to God as the head of his family.

From the beginning God has kept up with mankind by fathers as Biblical genealogies are listed by a father and their male offspring. One can read this in Numbers 26:2 when Moses took a census of Israel and divided land, both by their fathers.

> Take a census of all the males of the congregation of the Israelites by families, by their fathers' houses, according to the number of names, head by head. (Numbers 26:2 Amplified Bible)
>
> "But the land shall be divided by lot. They shall receive their inheritance according to the names of the tribes of their fathers. (Numbers 26:55 NASB)

At times females are mentioned in a Biblical genealogy, but for the most part readers we do not know mothers or daughters (Matthew 1:5, Numbers 26:33). A man's body produces male and female seed which determines gender, and both sexes are the recipients of their father's transference of iniquity.[3] We see this truth in the beginning of creation.

In Genesis 1:27, "God created man he him; male and female, created "he" "them." This scripture tells us "him" was male and female. The King James Bible brings this point out with living creatures.

> [21]And God created great whales, and every living creature that moveth, which the waters brought forth abundantly, after their kind, and every winged fowl after his kind: and God saw that it was good. (Genesis 1:21 KJV)
>
> [24]And God said, Let the earth bring forth the living creature after his kind, cattle, and creeping thing, and beast of the earth after his kind: and it was so. [25]And God made the beast of the earth after his kind, and cattle after their kind, and everything that creepeth upon the earth after his kind: and God saw that it was good. (Genesis 1:24-25 KJV)

Living creatures were made after "his" kind. Once God created a male, He followed with his female of like kind. A male set the pattern for his female, and in turn, he set the pattern for his offspring. Genesis chapter five states the same truth for humans. A male and female were called he, and he was a them, and both were called Adam. Both male and female were blessed to prosper by their Creator.[4]

Male and female created he them; and blessed them, and called their name Adam, in the day when they were created. (Genesis 5:2 KJV)

By this design of our Creator, a lineage of a male's family line can be traced back to the previous generations clearly through fathers, whose surname and Y chromosome pass to their sons as explained in this paragraph from the Human Genome Project. It seems God keeps track of humans through their fathers but did not leave mothers out by mitochondrial DNA (mtDNA).

"When DNA is passed from one generation to the next, most of it is mixed by the processes that make each person unique from his or her parents. Some special pieces of DNA, however, remain virtually unaltered as they pass from parent to child. One of these pieces is carried by the Y chromosome, which is passed only from father to son. Another piece, mitochondrial DNA (mtDNA), is passed (with few exceptions) only from mother to child. Since the DNA in the Y chromosome does not mix with other DNA, it is like a genetic surname that allows men to trace their paternal lineages. Similarly, mtDNA allows both men and women to trace their maternal lineages."[5]

The LORD [is] longsuffering, and of great mercy, forgiving iniquity and transgression, and by no means clearing [the guilty], visiting the iniquity of the fathers upon the children unto the third and fourth [generation]. (Numbers 14:18 KJV)

In Numbers 14:18 "visiting the iniquity of the fathers on the children to the third and the fourth generations," the word for "children" is ben in Hebrew. Notice in this verse it uses "fathers" as the focal point where the visitation of iniquity aims. Ben also means "a son or grandson as the builder of a family line and also can mean, children, both male and female."[6] Since "children" in this scripture was translated from ben, once again we see God's organization of family lines through fathers. The male is the builder of his family line, and iniquity transfers from him to his children, both male and female, then to the next generations.

Footnotes

[1] "sin." Collins English Dictionary - Complete & Unabridged 10th Edition. HarperCollins Publishers. <Dictionary. com. Jul 5, 2012.

[2] curse. Dictionary.com. Collins English Dictionary - Complete & Unabridged 10th Edition. HarperCollins Publishers. December 17, 2011.

[3] Exodus 34:6-7, Exodus 20:5, also Jeremiah

[4] Blue Letter Bible. "Dictionary and Word Search for Barak (Strong's 1288)". Blue Letter Bible. 1996-2012. Jul 17, 2012.

[5] Human Genome Project Human Migration. How do genes tell the story of our migration? January 12, 2012.

[6] Blue Letter Bible. "Dictionary and Word Search for '"son*" AND "H1121"' in the KJV". Blue Letter Bible. 1996-2012. Jan 11, 2012.

Chapter 6
Why Iniquity Transfers

You show unfailing love to thousands, but you also bring the consequences of one generation's sin upon the next. You are the great and powerful God, the LORD of Heaven's Armies. (Jeremiah 32:18 NLT)

God does not treat those who love him as their sins deserve, but sin still brings consequences (Psalms 103:10, Psalm 78:38). Recall in Numbers 14:18, iniquity is the same Hebrew word as in Exodus 34:7, avon, which means "perversity, depravity, guilt or consequence for iniquity."[1]

Numbers 14:18 and Exodus 34:7 contains a pinnacle statement that reveals the factor in iniquity that transfers to the next generations. In this verse, God "forgives iniquity and transgressions but he will by no means clear the guilty..." "By no means" is defined as "certainly not, not by any means."[2] The Gesenius Hebrew-Chaldee Lexicon defines iniquity (avon) in Exodus 34:7 as "the guilt of the fathers."[3]

This statement tells us the Lord will certainly not clear the guilt of the fathers. Guilt seeks a transfer to the next generations (Exodus 14:18). This spiritual truth still is at work today, even in the lives of Christians. How could this be? Christians were once sinners, who have parents and those in previous generations who sinned. These iniquities will visit, seeking to remain in the family through evil spirits. Turning to the Lord in repentance provides the blood of Jesus, and the only way guilt becomes forgiven.

Chapter 7
Guilt's Flow

> He by no means clears the guilty, visiting the iniquity of the fathers on the children to the third and fourth generation. (Numbers 14:18b NKJV)

"The guilty, visiting" is one Hebrew word paqad (Strong's H6485).[1] Paqad occurs two times in the King James Bible, Exodus 34:7 and Numbers 14:18.

Of course, the word "guilty" involves guilt. It is the guilt of the guilty in one's family line that allows iniquity to visit the next generations. "I forgive iniquity, rebellion, and sin. But I do not excuse the guilty. I lay the sins of the parents upon their children and grandchildren; the entire family is affected, even children in the third and fourth generations." (Exodus 34:5-7 NLT) Iniquity's purpose is to permeate and take over as it did through Lucifer.

Sin was inherited and guilt came with it. Guilt is hereditary as well and the factor that allows iniquity to tempt the next generation. We inherited guilt from Adam. For example, after Adam sinned, his children who came after him did not eat the forbidden fruit. Nonetheless, his offspring inherited the same iniquity as Adam. Adam and Eve transgressed by revolting from God's word, but the generations to come did not do it. Even so, they share the same consequence from the guilt of sin: death. (Rom 5:12;14 NLT)

The guilt of iniquity visits the next generations to set a trap in order to reproduce itself. In Jeremiah 11:9-10, this process becomes illuminated. "And the LORD said to me, "A conspiracy has been found among the men of Judah and among the inhabitants of Jerusalem." (Jeremiah 11:9 NKJV) The Revised Standard Bible states "There is revolt among the men of Judah and the inhabitants of Jerusalem." (Jeremiah 11:9 RSV) Instead of conspiracy, the word "revolt" is used. A revolt from God's word threw them into the same iniquity trap of their predecessors.

> "They have turned back to the iniquities of their forefathers who refused to hear My words, and they have gone after other gods to serve them; the house of Israel and the house of Judah have broken My covenant which I made with their father." (Jeremiah 11:10 NKJV)

Israel entered the promised land but did not listen to do what the Lord commanded. The generation that came out of Egypt, led by Moses, died in the desert because they did the same thing. God spoke, and they revolted from his word. They did not trust God after all the miracles he performed to get them out of Egypt. The consequences came upon them. Iniquity's flow will catch anyone who does as they did (Deuteronomy 1:19-45).

Footnote
[1] "H6485"- `paqad' - Strong's Hebrew Lexicon (KJV)." Blue Letter Bible. Web. 6 Feb 2020.

Chapter 8
Guilt Train

Guilt from the Old Testament occurred when someone broke the law of God.

> "For whoever keeps the whole law and yet stumbles at just one point is guilty of breaking all of it." (James 2:10 NIV)

God provided rules for mankind's conduct by giving the Ten Commandments (Exodus 20) along with the first five books of the Bible (Pentateuch). God's standards are far greater than sinful man can carry out.

According to scripture, guilt occurs through both intentional (Leviticus 6:1-4) and unintentional sin (Leviticus 4:22, 5:17). King David stated, "You, God, know my folly; my guilt is not hidden from you" (Psalm 69:5 NIV). God is aware of everyone's guilt, and how it came about.

After King David did what he knew in his heart was wrong, his conscience began to bother him. And he said to the LORD, "I have sinned greatly by taking this census. Please forgive my guilt, LORD, for doing this foolish thing" (2 Samuel 24:10 NLT). Guilt brings heaviness to one's conscience as it did David.

> Therefore, just as through one man sin entered the world, and death through sin, and thus death spread to all men, because all sinned. (Romans 5:12 NKJV)

Sin and guilt offerings were established by God as a means to atone for sin by the sprinkled blood of animal sacrifice (Leviticus 17:11). Guilt follows the bloodline, and by the sprinkling of innocent blood, guilt was appeased.

> And according to the law almost all things are purified with blood, and without shedding of blood there is no remission. (Hebrews 9:22 NKJV)

The blood of animals did not please God. It covered sin until the time of Jesus. His sacrificial death on the cross satisfied God's need for justice through his blood (Hebrews 10:1-12). Jesus provided the only way out of the iniquity trap.

Chapter 9
Enticed To Sin

From one generation to the next, guilt of sin allows iniquity to repeat. God's word and its importance must be considered, for the problem is spiritual and physical (Isaiah 55:11). Sin comes through lustful desire arising from a person's own fallen nature. Everyone has his or her own forte for sin. However, iniquity comes along from prior generations to seek a path as well.

Iniquity finds its pathway through evil spirits who work alongside family lines. They initiate the repetition of sin in the generations. In the same way angels are assigned to individuals, so evil spirits work through families to repeat iniquity.

An evil spirit may be identified by the condition it brings or the result of its presence according to the example Jesus gave us (Luke 8:30, Luke 11:14). In Luke 8:30, Jesus asked the ruling spirit within a man his name. A name identifies a particular person, and by his or her name a person is recognized. A name brings identity and description to a spirit as well.

> And Jesus asked him, "What is your name?" And he said, "Legion"; for many demons had entered him. (Luke 8:30 NASB)
>
> And He was casting out a demon, and it was mute; when the demon had gone out, the mute man spoke; and the crowds were amazed. (Luke 11:14 NASB)

Chapter 10
Repetition in Iniquity

Look again at Numbers 14:18 and the phrase "visiting the iniquity." Visit means "to go to," so iniquity of a father visits, or goes to, every one of his children, grandchildren, and great grandchildren.1 The visit seeks to transfer the sin of a father onto the next generations. This may extend beyond the third and fourth generation if a father engages the iniquity and passes it on to repeat the process. Recall mothers are not excluded, but one must look to her father to see the iniquity flow which moves through both sexes to affect his generations.

A natural way iniquity repeats from one generation to the next comes by contact with our families. In our day, two to three generations, and possibly more, of a family line may be alive at once. When family members are around one another, they become accustomed to each other's way of life. Such closeness in families makes it easy for members to observe behaviors, either right or wrong, and copy them. This similarly occurs with anyone else you spend time with, along with any activities. You can see how sins and iniquities may easily pass through these generations.

For example, iniquity may transfer to our children through family beliefs and life choices. The alcoholic says, "I drink because I am under pressure of responsibility" or "I drink because life has been so cruel to me." The adulterer says, "I cheat because my spouse is uncaring." Since individuals act out of what they believe, strongholds can develop leading to sin. Iniquity may then gain a foothold in the next generation.

What about a child who does not know his or her biological family? It does not matter. This is a spiritual law, and iniquity of the fathers will still visit that child. God set spiritual precedence for mankind by his Word, and any violation authorizes iniquity to pass on to the generations. The kingdom of darkness keeps iniquity moving from the spirit realm.

From one generation to the next, a transition of how iniquity plays out may occur, depending on the individuals and the choices they make. If a man steals, then that visits his children, grandchildren, and great grandchildren; each one may become a thief or some other kind of criminal. Or maybe they are an undetected thief. Nevertheless, iniquity seeks a way to work. Additionally, this sin opens the door for anyone in this family line to be victimized by such activity due to iniquity passed on from ancestors.

Another example of the repetition of iniquity took place when the crowd condemned Jesus to death. Their words reveal an understanding of the concept of iniquity's flow.

> "Why? What crime has he committed?" asked Pilate. But they shouted all the louder, "Crucify him!" 24 When Pilate saw that he was getting nowhere, but that instead an uproar was starting, he took water and washed his hands in front of the crowd. "I am innocent of this man's blood," he said. "It is your responsibility!" 25 All the people answered, "His blood is on us and on our children!" (Matthew 27:23-25 NIV)

The crowd demanded Jesus to be executed, even though Pilate declared his innocence. (Luke 23:13-16) Then the crowd emphatically passed their guilt onto their children. How ironic, the Lamb of God who willingly gave himself to break the power of iniquity, stood before this crowd who willingly released iniquity upon themselves and their children.

Chapter 11
King David's Iniquity

A Biblical example of iniquity and the different ways it played out in a family line can be observed in the life of King David. We begin with his sexual sin of adultery. "But the thing that David had done was evil in the sight of the LORD." (2 Samuel 11:27b NASB)

On one occasion "when King's go to war," David chose not to go and remained at his palace (2 Samuel 11:1). The king sent his army to battle without him. This proves to be a very poor decision on his part. One evening he could not sleep. Maybe his mind stayed on his army far away. Little did he know iniquity prepared a trap. "Then it happened one evening that David arose from his bed and walked on the roof of the king's house. And from the roof he saw a woman bathing, and the woman was very beautiful to behold." (2 Samuel 11:2 KJV)

Who was she? He wanted to know. "So, David sent and inquired about the woman. And [someone] said, "[Is] this not Bathsheba, the daughter of Eliam, the wife of Uriah the Hittite?" (2 Samuel 11:3 NKJV) Lust seized David. The king sent for her even after he knew she was married. Not only married, but her father and husband were apart of David's mighty men who served him faithfully (2 Samuel 33:34, 2 Samuel 12).

King David took Uriah the Hittite's wife for sex who became pregnant. He then arranged her husband's murder to hide the adultery. Once Uriah was killed, King David married Bathsheba. David had other wives; he did not need to take another man's wife. He stepped into the iniquity trap acquired from his forefathers. David revolted from doing the right thing. He could have turned his head and gone to bed alone. His uncontrolled lust motivated him as iniquity took him further than sex with a married woman. His guilt did not miss God's attention.

> 9 'Why have you despised the word of the LORD by doing evil in His sight? You have struck down Uriah the Hittite with the sword, have taken his wife to be your wife, and have killed him with the sword of the sons of Ammon. 10 'Now therefore, the sword shall never depart from your house, because you have despised Me and have taken the wife of Uriah the Hittite to be your wife.' 11"Thus says the LORD, 'Behold, I will raise up evil against you from your own household; I will even take your wives before your eyes and give them to your companion, and he will lie with your wives in broad daylight. 12'Indeed you did it secretly, but I will do this thing before all Israel and under the sun.'" 13Then David said to Nathan, "I have sinned against the LORD." And Nathan said to David, "The LORD also has taken away your sin; you shall not die. 14"However, because by this deed you have given occasion to the enemies of the LORD to blaspheme, the child also that is born to you shall surely die." (2 Samuel 12:9-14 NASB)

With nothing hidden before God, David did not get away with anything. In Psalm 38 King David described the weight of guilt which he carried from iniquities.

> For mine iniquities are gone over mine head: as a heavy burden they are too heavy for me. (Psalm 38:4 KJV)
>
> My guilt has overwhelmed me like a burden too heavy to bear. (Psalm 38:4 NIV)

An important key for King David, once confronted with his sin, he repented. After King David's death, God referred to him as "My servant David whom I chose, who observed My commandments and My statutes" (1 Kings 11:34).

But this did not stop iniquity that gained access to his family line (2 Samuel 12:13). Consequences of his sins were declared to King David by Nathan, a prophet of God, and it was not good. "The sword would never leave his house, evil would rise up against King David from his household, his wives would be taken, and one close would have sex with them in broad daylight, and the son conceived in the act of adultery would die." (2 Samuel 12:9-14)

Now let's add to our study another Psalm written by King David which proves to be revealing. "A Psalm of David, when Nathan the prophet went to him, after he had gone into Bathsheba. Have mercy on me, O God, according to your steadfast love; according to your abundant mercy blot out my transgressions. Wash me thoroughly from my iniquity and cleanse me from my sin! For I know my transgressions, and my sin is ever before me. (Psalm 51:1-3 ESV) King David asked God to remove his transgressions, iniquity, and then his sin (Psalm 51:4 ESV).

Chapter 12
Brother by Another Mother?

King David fell into the iniquity trap. So, let's dig into his family heritage using what we've learned thus far. A statement by King David stands out strongly to me: "I was brought forth in iniquity. (Psalm 51:5).

> "Behold, I was brought forth in iniquity, and in sin did my mother conceive me." (Psalm 51:5 (ESV)

I previously read Psalms 51:5 as a blanket statement that as David, all are born as sinners. Not this time, David said, "I was shapen in iniquity; and in sin my mother conceived me." (Psalm 51:5 KJV)

The Amplified Bible states, "I was brought forth in [a state of] wickedness; In sin my mother conceived me [and from my beginning I, too, was sinful]." (Psalm 51:5 Amplified Bible)

He states that his conception came out of sin as a product of iniquity. I did not say this. King David did. What was King David talking about? David understood something about his conception that troubled him.

Since iniquity follows the father's family line, to David's father we turn. Obviously, David had to be told about the circumstances of his conception. David was the youngest son of Jesse.

> 13 Jesse begot Eliab his firstborn, Abinadab the second, Shimea the third, 14 Nethanel the fourth, Raddai the fifth, 15 Ozem the sixth, and David the seventh. (1 Chronicles 2:13-15 NKJV)

1 Chronicles provides a list of Jesse's seven sons in order of birth. 1 Samuel 17:12 states that Jesse was the father of eight sons. Only seven sons of Jesse appeared before the prophet Samuel. On this occasion God told the prophet to anoint one of Jesse's sons as the next king. All Jesse's sons were invited but David (1 Samuel 16:7). Doesn't that sound strange? From here let's read another statement from King David.

> For it is for your sake that I have borne reproach, that dishonor has covered my face.8 I have become a stranger to my brothers, an alien to my mother's sons." (Psalm 69:7-8 ESV).

Now to add a few different translations to see what we can find.

> "I am become a stranger unto my brethren, and an alien unto my mother's children." (Psalm 69:8 KJV)

> "Even my own brothers pretend they don't know me; they treat me like a stranger." (Psalm 69:8 NLT)

"My own brothers treat me like a stranger; they act as if I were a foreigner." (Psalm 69:8 NET).

As he grew up, disdain seemed to be prevalent in the relationship with David's brothers and possibly with his father. His father Jesse did not even bother to get David from tending the sheep when the prophet Samuel requested to meet with all his sons. The Lord sent Samuel to anoint the next king, which happened to be David. (1 Samuel 16). Why would Jesse intentionally exclude his youngest son from such meeting with the prophet?

Another example of family dynamics occurred when David brought supplies to his brothers in Saul's army. It happened to be the time when Goliath taunted Israel's army.

> And Eliab his eldest brother heard when he spake unto the men; and Eliab's anger was kindled against David, and he said, Why camest thou down hither? and with whom hast thou left those few sheep in the wilderness? I know thy pride, and the naughtiness of thine heart; for thou art come down that thou mightiest see the battle. And David said, "What have I now done? [Is there] not a cause?" (Samuel 17:29 KJV)

"Now what have I done?" said David, "Can't I even speak?" (Samuel 17:29 NIV)

This again displays his relationship with his oldest brother. 1 Chronicles reveals a key to understanding this attitude of David's brothers. Hold on, this is going to get interesting. Was King David Jesse's son by a different mother than his brothers? This prospect seems to be feasible. 1 Chronicles 2:13-15 gave us the names of Jesse's sons. The next verse adds more information about David's family. As we continue in 1 Chronicles chapter 2, we realize David also had two sisters.

> 16 And their sisters were Zeruiah and Abigail. The sons of Zeruiah: Abishai, Joab, and Asahel, three… (1 Chronicles 2:16)

It says that "their sisters were Zeruiah and Abigail." It does not state these sisters were Jesse's daughters (1 Chronicles 2:16 ESV). In this case, we turn back to the Bible for answers.

> And Absalom made Amasa captain of the host instead of Joab: which Amasa [was] a man's son, whose name [was] Ithra an Israelite, that went into Abigail the daughter of Nahash, sister to Zeruiah Joab's mother. (2 Samuel 17:25 KJV)

Indeed, these sisters of David were not Jesse's biological daughters. David's sisters were Zeruiah and Abigail. Nahash was listed as the father of "Abigail and Zeruiah". Nahash conceived daughters with David's mother. Sometimes afterwards, Jesse and she conceived David. There are different scenarios concerning David's conception, so let's look at them.

The Bible does not mention King David's mother by name. A Jewish legend has named her Nitzevet, but there is no biblical confirmation of that name. David's father, Jesse, lived in Bethlehem and was from the tribe of Judah. But we don't have much information on David's mother other than she was a godly woman. In one of David's psalms, he prays, "Save me, because I serve you just as my mother did." (Psalm 86:16)

Nahash was an Ammonite king (1 Samuel 11:1). Speculation suggests that David's mother had been married to Nahash when she bore the half-sisters and then later became the second wife of Jesse. Further speculation implies that David's mother was not yet married to Jesse when she became pregnant—that perhaps she was still married to Nahash when she conceived David.

> "In Jewish tradition, David's mother was Nitzevet, the daughter of Adael and the wife of Jesse. The Talmud relates a complicated story concerning Nitzevet. Her husband, Jesse, began to doubt the purity of his ancestry, since he was the grandson of Ruth the Moabitess (Ruth 4:17). Due to his doubts, Jesse stopped having marital relations with Nitzevet after she had borne her seventh son. Instead, Jesse planned to marry his Canaanite servant and have children with her. The maidservant, however, had pity on Nitzevet and offered Nitzevet a plan: On the wedding night, Nitzevet and the maidservant could secretly switch places, and Nitzevet could sleep with Jesse one more time. The switch worked, much as Leah and Rachel's switch had worked on Jacob, and Nitzevet became pregnant with David, her eighth son. Nitzevet never revealed to Jesse what she had done, even when her pregnancy was apparent. Therefore, Nitzevet came to be despised as an immoral woman, and her son David grew up an outcast in his own family. Again, this is an extrabiblical legend, and there is no way to confirm the accuracy of the tale of Nitzevet".[1]

In David's own words he called his conception "one of iniquity" from Psalms 51:5. Iniquity is the same Hebrew word avon. David believed the circumstances of his conception were a result of iniquity and sin.

Recall that "the guilty, visiting" spiritual law releases a visit of guilt to the next generation. How did Jesse come in contact with David's mother whose daughters Abigail and Zeruiah were fathered by an Ammorite king? If Jesse impregnated David's mother while she was still married to Nashash, this would be similar to King David's sexual encounter with Bathsheba. David heard about his conception whether by the scenario with Nitzevet or another man's wife who conceived a son. The manner in which David was treated by his family reminded him as well. If his mother was another man's wife, David took iniquity further when he arranged Uriah's death to hide his sin and then married his wife.

Footnote

[1] "Does the Bible mention David's mother?" Got Questions.org. Iniquity in David's Family

CHAPTER 13
INIQUITY IN DAVID'S FAMILY

How did iniquity actually play out in King David's family line? His children's lives tell the story. King David's sin with Bathsheba began as a sexual transgression. With Numbers 14:18 in mind, iniquity visits "on" the children. On is a preposition meaning "to be attached or unified with; in connection, association, or cooperation with."[1]

With an opened door of sexual transgressions from King David, iniquity found a way into the next generation after him. Tamar, one of King David's virgin daughters, was raped by her half-brother.

> 11But as she was feeding him, he grabbed her and demanded, "Come to bed with me, my darling sister."12"No, my brother!" she cried. "Don't be foolish! Don't do this to me! Such wicked things aren't done in Israel. 13Where could I go in my shame? And you would be called one of the greatest fools in Israel. Please, just speak to the king about it, and he will let you marry me." 14But Amnon wouldn't listen to her, and since he was stronger than she was, he raped her. (1 Samuel 13:11-14 NLT)

Tamar begged Amnon to stop his assault.; She did not want such shame upon her (2 Samuel 13). Tamar had done nothing wrong, but iniquity seized Amnon to move through and struck King David's next generation. Amnon victimized and then despised his sister, which forever changed her life.

> 15Then suddenly Amnon's love turned to hate, and he hated her even more than he had loved her. "Get out of here!" he snarled at her.16"No, no!" Tamar cried. "Sending me away now is worse than what you've already done to me." But Amnon wouldn't listen to her. 17He shouted for his servant and demanded, "Throw this woman out, and lock the door behind her!" 18So the servant put her out and locked the door behind her. She was wearing a long, beautiful robe, as was the custom in those days for the king's virgin daughters. 19But now Tamar tore her robe and put ashes on her head. And then, with her face in her hands, she went away crying.20Her brother Absalom saw her and asked, "Is it true that Amnon has been with you? Well, my sister, keep quiet for now, since he's your brother. Don't you worry about it?" So, Tamar lived as a desolate woman in her brother Absalom's house. 21When King David heard what had happened, he was very angry. 22And though Absalom never spoke to Amnon about this, he hated Amnon deeply because of what he had done to his sister. (2 Samuel 13:15-22 NLT)

The second phase of King David's sin with Bathsheba involved murder, with the arranged death of Bathsheba's husband. Similarly, Tamar's brother Absalom, another son of King David, plotted to have Amnon killed in revenge for the rape of his sister Tamar (2 Samuel 13:32).

> 23Two years later, when Absalom's sheep were being sheared at Baal-hazor near Ephraim, Absalom invited all the king's sons to come to a feast. 24He went to the king and said, "My sheep-shearers are now at work. Would the king and his servants please come to celebrate the occasion with me?" 25The king replied, "No, my son. If we all came, we would be too much of a burden on you." Absalom pressed him, but the king would not come, though he gave Absalom his blessing. 26"Well, then," Absalom said, "if you can't come, how about sending my brother Amnon with us?" "Why Amnon?" the king asked. 27But Absalom kept on pressing the king until he finally agreed to let all his sons attend, including Amnon. So, Absalom prepared a feast fit for a king. 28Absalom told his men, "Wait until Amnon gets drunk; then at my signal, kill him! Don't be afraid. I'm the one who has given the command. Take courage and do it!" 29So at Absalom's signal they murdered Amnon. (2 Samuel 13:23-28 NLT)

It was also Absolom who committed adultery with his father's concubines as Nathan the prophet declared. A tent was pitched so all Israel would know, which brought public shame to King David in broad daylight. King David tried to hide his sins, so adultery committed against him was openly displayed. His own children were evildoers against his house (I Samuel 16:21-22).

This generation after King David made iniquity's path quite easy. All this occurred because of the spiritual law stated in Numbers 14:18 and Exodus 34:7.

We have not mentioned King Solomon, but iniquity from his father definitely worked against him and brought his downfall. Iniquity came in a similar fashion as his father, lust of the flesh. This iniquity trap pulled King Solomon away from following the ways of the Lord (1 Kings 3:3). Not one woman, not two, nor three would do, but many.

> "Now King Solomon loved many foreign women, along with the daughter of Pharaoh: Moabite, Ammonite, Edomite, Sidonian, and Hittite women, from the nations concerning which the LORD had said to the people of Israel, "You shall not enter into marriage with them, neither shall they with you, for surely they will turn away your heart after their gods." Solomon clung to these in love. He had 700 wives, who were princesses, and 300 concubines. And his wives turned away his heart. 4 For when Solomon was old his wives turned away his heart after other gods, and his heart was not wholly true to the LORD his God, as was the heart of David his father." (1 Kings 11:1-4 ESV)

What entrapped such a wise man? Plainly, sexual relationships with women from the nations God forbade Israel from marrying. (Nehemiah 13:26)

Solomon, a man declared to have wisdom and discernment like none before or after him, yielded to the iniquity prevalent in his family line. His uncontrolled sexual desire perverted the command of God (1 Kings 11:2). Solomon allowed iniquity to take him further than the previous generation by turning his heart from the Lord.

Now back to comprehend how iniquity gained access to Amnon, let's back up to find out what happened.

1Now David's son Absalom had a beautiful sister named Tamar. And Amnon, her half-brother, fell desperately in love with her. 2 Amnon became so obsessed with Tamar that he became ill. She was a virgin, and Amnon thought he could never have her.3But Amnon had a very crafty friend—his cousin Jonadab. He was the son of David's brother Shimea. 4One day Jonadab said to Amnon, "What's the trouble? Why should the son of a king look so dejected morning after morning?" So, Amnon told him, "I am in love with Tamar, my brother Absalom's sister."5"Well," Jonadab said, "I'll tell you what to do. Go back to bed and pretend you are ill. When your father comes to see you, ask him to let Tamar come and prepare some food for you. Tell him you'll feel better if she prepares it as you watch and feeds you with her own hands." (2 Samuel 13:1-5 NLT)

Verse 2 is a key: Amnon became obsessed with having sex with Tamar to the point of illness. Temptation arose from his own lust which Amnon did not control and allowed to get stronger. Maybe he replayed over and over in his mind what it would be like to have sex with her. Iniquity kept knocking at the door of his heart. Then, finally, Amnon shared his lustful desire with a "crafty friend" who happened to be his cousin. Crafty means "Skillful in underhand or evil schemes; cunning; deceitful; sly," which indicated evil influence from a person who gave Amnon wicked advice. The word "crafty" described Satan in the Garden of Eden before the fall of Adam and Eve. Satan, an evil spirit, enticed Adam and Eve to sin via the serpent. So crafty advice was just what the devil ordered to gain access to King David's offspring. This advice made the way for iniquity to be passed on to them.[2]

He who sows iniquity will reap sorrow, And the rod of his anger will fail. (Proverbs 22:8 NKJV)

Iniquity's ploy to seize Absalom as a vessel likewise came by way of foolish advice. This advice came at a time when Absalom sought to take the throne from his father. King David prayed that Ahithophel's advice to Absalom would be foolishness, but interestingly, it was that foolish advice that persuaded Absalom's public display of sexual immorality with his father's concubines (2 Samuel 15

20 Then Absalom turned to Ahithophel and asked him, "What should I do next?" 21Ahithophel told him, "Go and sleep with your father's concubines, for he has left them here to look after the palace. Then all Israel will know that you have insulted your father beyond hope of reconciliation, and they will throw their support to you." 22So they set up a tent on the palace roof where everyone could see it, and Absalom went in and had sex with his father's concubines. 23Absalom followed Ahithophel's advice, just as David had done. For every word Ahithophel spoke seemed as wise as though it had come directly from the mouth of God. (2 Samuel 16:20-23 NLT).

Iniquity mandates visits upon the children to repeat the sins of their father's. Recall iniquity began with Satan and sought to continue its hold on the generations. Both Amnon and Absalom transgressed into sexual sin, and both were killed, a reflection of King David's sin and iniquities.

Iniquity in the line of King David and the mothers of his children produced an open door. David produced an Absolom and a Tamar. One who yielded to the iniquity trap and sinned. The other an innocent victim of the one who yielded.

> 8For the battle there was spread over the whole countryside, and the forest devoured more people that day than the sword devoured. 9Now Absalom happened to meet the servants of David. For Absalom was riding on [his] mule, and the mule went under the thick branches of a great oak. And his head caught fast in the oak, so he was left hanging between heaven and earth, while the mule that was under him kept going. 10When a certain man saw [it], he told Joab and said, "Behold, I saw Absalom hanging in an oak." 11Then Joab said to the man who had told him, "Now behold, you saw [him]! Why then did you not strike him there to the ground? And I would have given you ten [pieces] of silver and a belt." 12The man said to Joab, "Even if I should receive a thousand [pieces of] silver in my hand, I would not put out my hand against the king's son; for in our hearing the king charged you and Abishaiand Ittai, saying, Protect for me the young man Absalom!' 13"Otherwise, if I had dealt treacherously against his life (and there is nothing hidden from the king), then you yourself would have stood aloof." 14Then Joab said, "I will not waste time here with you." So he took three spears in his hand and thrust them through the heart of Absalom while he was yet alive in the midst of the oak. 15And ten young men who carried Joab's armor gathered around and struck Absalom and killed him. (2 Samuel 18:8-15 NASB)

Footnotes

[1] "on". Dictionary.com Unabridged. Random House, Inc. <Dictionary.com

[2] "crafty." Dictionary.com Unabridged. Random House, Inc. <Dictionary.com

Chapter 14
Victims of Iniquity

We found with the first iniquity transfer to humans, Satan lured, Adam and Eve into a sin trap. Caught by ignoring God's command, they became his victims. Victim defined, 1) "a person who suffers from a destructive or injurious action or agency. 2) a person who is deceived or cheated, as by his or her own emotions or ignorance, by the dishonesty of others, or by some impersonal agency".[1]

When iniquity transfers it may come by an individual victimizing another person or persons. Just as with Able, Tamar, David's wives (raped by Absalom), all were victims of the actions of another person. Additionally, recall victimization can transfer in a family line. In all three of these cases, sin followed the path of iniquity.

Furthermore, look for victimization within one's own family line. Has anyone been sexually molested by a family member or another individual? This creates abusers and victims who may become an abuser themselves. Many times, this remains hidden and unknown. Understanding iniquity hopefully will help us further discern events in our lives and put an end to iniquity cycles.

Footnote

[1] "victim" Dictionary.com Unabridged based on the random House Unabridged Dictionary @ Random House, Inc. 2023.

Chapter 15
The Visit

Could it be that God is looking for someone in a family line to repent and turn to him in order to deal with the iniquity problem? I believe this to be so. After all God stated he was compassionate and merciful (Micah 17:18-19). He is looking for someone to reset a family line. This does not mean that iniquity in a family line will not tempt a person into the same sin as his forefathers. Just like in the temptation of Jesus in the desert, the tempter came to Jesus when he was weak. Why at that point? He sought to seize the moment to destroy him. If Jesus had not withstood him, we all would have been lost.

Look again at Numbers 14:18 and the phrase "visiting the iniquity." Visit means "to go to," so iniquity of a father visits, or goes to, every one of his children, grandchildren, and great grandchildren. The visit seeks to transfer guilt through sin of a father onto the next generations. This may extend beyond the third and fourth generation if a father engages the iniquity and passes it on to repeat the process.[1] Recall mothers are not excluded, but one must look to her father for iniquity's flow. But do examine the sins of mothers to discover iniquity from her bloodline.

Iniquity visits the next generation looking for a host. Iniquity is a violation of God's law. The visit of iniquity seeks to bring upon the next generation the same types of transgressions. If one is not aware of this, the visit of iniquity proves successful.

Iniquity recreates similar circumstances from one generation to another. It makes it easy for the next generation to step into the same bondage as the previous generation. For example, take hoarding. How much stuff is enough? If one's parents or grandparents were hoarders, watch out.

Think about this. Can one generation instill their prejudices or offenses into the next? Absolutely! This would provide another example of how iniquity moves through family lines.

> "Keeping mercy and lovingkindness for thousands, forgiving iniquity and transgression and sin; but He will by no means leave the guilty unpunished, visiting (avenging) the iniquity (sin, guilt) of the fathers upon the children and the grandchildren to the third and fourth generations [that is, calling the children to account for the sins of their fathers]." (Exodus 34:7)

The visit comes externally by a spirit familiar with the iniquity in a person's family line. It follows the bloodline. A spirit visits and operates similarly as Satan tempted Jesus. It twists truth, tempts the lust of the flesh, eyes, and the pride of life, just as it did with Jesus. The visit's purpose. To entice one to sin. Jesus defeated Satan, but scripture said he would return to Jesus for a more opportune time (Luke 4:13 NIV). Another opportune time would be an example of an additional visit to entice one into an iniquity trap.

Chapter 16
Adopted Children and Iniquity

Adopted children and their parents need to be aware of the iniquity trap. Iniquity from your child's bloodline will seek a way to function even though they're adopted. For example, if a child comes out of chaotic family dynamics, this iniquity seeks to recreate chaos in their life. This can affect the adoptive family or any future home. Most adoptive parents are not aware of how iniquity works. I suggest finding out about your child's biological parents, if possible. This may help your child avoid similar problems.

What to Do

Train up a child in the way he should go: and when he is old, he will not depart from it. Proverbs 22:6 (KJV)

Adoptive parents must pray for their children as any parent. Ask the Lord to reveal what iniquity flows in the bloodline of your child if you do not know. With this information, watch for these types of behavior. Address negative behavior wisely when it occurs. Your child must learn right from wrong. When your adopted son or daughter grows up, you might see iniquities in their lives. Do not worry, continue to pray. If you trained your child in the ways of the Lord, the promise of this scripture stands. "He will not depart from righteous training "when he is old. (Proverbs 22:6) Believe God to fulfill this word, he will do it.

Chapter 17
When a Generation Dies

As your parents pass away, especially the last parent, be watchful. Iniquity seeks to remain in the family. Iniquity wants to keep the same sin patterns operating from one generation to the next.

When the last surviving parent dies, grief, sorrow, and sadness abound. Then, while still in mourning, the chore of dealing with the family estate arises. On this occasion, unhealed wounds among siblings as well as other family dynamics may be triggered. Even offenses from childhood may surface. Some children naturally fight when growing up. Strongholds can exist when unhealed emotional wounds remain in a person. In these strongholds, a demonic spirit can hide. These spirits seek a perpetual iniquity trap to remain in a family line if able to do so (2 Corinthians 10:4).

> "In your anger do not sin. Do not let the sun go down while you are still angry" (Ephesians 4:26).

Please be aware of this when dealing with the death of your last parent. Watch out for raw emotions of family wounds or bondages. Walk in awareness and forgiveness of one another. Seek unity through peace, but do not forget what iniquity is up to.

When you find yourself going through the death of your last parent, keep your spiritual discernment alert. Take note of what types of sins manifest and how it operates among your family. Then be vigilant to stand against it in your life.

Chapter 18
Iniquity of Scribes and Pharisees

One day Jesus bluntly addressed the scribes and the Pharisees concerning their hypocrisy. In this direct discourse, Jesus spoke of the flow of iniquity from their fathers. He began with Cain, who murdered his righteous brother, then Jesus spoke of their fathers who murdered Zechariah (Matthew 23:35 NKJV).

> "Woe to you, scribes and Pharisees, hypocrites! For you are like whitewashed tombs which indeed appear beautiful outwardly, but inside are full of dead [men's] bones and all uncleanness. 28 "Even so you also outwardly appear righteous to men, but inside you are full of hypocrisy and lawlessness. 29 "Woe to you, scribes and Pharisees, hypocrites! Because you build the tombs of the prophets and adorn the monuments of the righteous, 30 "and say, 'If we had lived in the days of our fathers, we would not have been partakers with them in the blood of the prophets.' 31"Therefore you are witnesses against yourselves that you are sons of those who murdered the prophets. 32 "Fill up, then, the measure of your fathers' [guilt.]. (Matthew 23:27-32 NKJV)

This is iniquity! Jesus was not done. He revealed these men would indeed repeat the iniquity of their fathers.

> 33"Serpents, brood of vipers! How can you escape the condemnation of hell? 34" Therefore I am sending you prophets and sages and teachers. Some of them you will kill and crucify; others you will flog in your synagogues and pursue from town to town. 35"that on you may come all the righteous blood shed on the earth, from the blood of righteous Abel to the blood of Zechariah, son of Berechiah, whom you murdered between the temple and the altar. (Matthew 23:33-35 NKJV)

The same type of persecution and murder continued to repeat throughout the generations of these men. As a result, Jesus said, 35" So all the righteous blood shed on the earth will be charged to you, from the blood of righteous Abel to the blood of Zechariah, son of Berechiah, whom you murdered between the sanctuary and the altar." (Matthew 23:35 CSB) There are heavy consequences to iniquity outside of the mercy of God.

Chapter 19
Jesus Defeats Iniquity

Satan visited Jesus with the same trap that caught and ensnared Adam. The trap set for Jesus, temptation to rebel through disobedience to God's word.

> Then Jesus was led by the Spirit into the wilderness to be tempted by the devil. 2 After fasting forty days and forty nights, he was hungry.3 The tempter came to him and said, "If you are the Son of God, tell these stones to become bread."4 Jesus answered, "It is written: 'Man shall not live on bread alone, but on every word that comes from the mouth of God.'" (Matthew 4:1-4 NASB)

Satan sought to entrap Jesus at first by the lust of the flesh. After 40 days of not eating, bread seemed like a good way to entice the son of man, but it didn't work.

Even though hungry, Jesus stood on God's word. He countered Satan's temptation with the spoken Word of God. Yet, the temptation of Jesus continued. Then Satan tried the lust of the eyes, then lastly the pride of life.

> 5 Then the devil took him to the holy city and had him stand on the highest point of the temple. 6 "If you are the Son of God," he said, "throw yourself down. For it is written: 'He will command his angels concerning you and they will lift you up in their hands so that you will not strike your foot against a stone."7 Jesus answered him, "It is also written: 'Do not put the Lord your God to the test.'" Matthew 4:5-7 NASB

Jesus did not fall to Satan's deceptive words. What could have taken place if Jesus did what Satan requested? Well simply put, he could have died prematurely, forfeiting the cross. Jesus defeated Satan by his knowledge and correct use of God's word. Satan's tactic worked so well to ensnare Eve and then Adam, but not Jesus (Genesis 3:1-6).

> 8 Again, the devil took him to a very high mountain and showed him all the kingdoms of the world and their splendor. "All this I will give you," he said, "if you will bow down and worship me."10 Jesus said to him, "Away from me, Satan! For it is written: 'Worship the Lord your God and serve him only.'"11 Then the devil left him, and angels came and attended him." (Matthew 4:8-11 NASB)

How does Satan entice people into sin? "Each person is tempted when they are dragged away by their own evil desire and enticed. Then, after desire has conceived, it gives birth to sin; and sin, when it is full-grown, gives birth to death." (James 1:14-15 NASB)

Jesus needed to defeat iniquity for himself and for us. He did so as a man empowered by the Holy Spirit. Jesus resisted temptation and prevailed. "For we do not have a high priest who is unable to empathize with our weaknesses, but we have one who has been tempted in every way, just as we are-- yet he did not sin." (Hebrews 4:14)

To defeat iniquity, one must resist temptation just as Jesus demonstrated. Submission to God and his word comes first, then resisting the temptation comes next. "Submit yourselves, then, to God. Resist the devil, and he will flee from you." (James 4:7 NIV)

God even promises help and a way out when tempted. "No temptation has overtaken you except what is common to mankind. And God is faithful; he will not let you be tempted beyond what you can bear. But when you are tempted, he will also provide a way out so that you can endure it." (1 Corinthians 13-15)

Footnotes:

Matthew 4:1 The Greek for tempted can also mean tested.

Matthew 4:4 Deut. 8:3

Matthew 4:6 Psalm 91:11, 12

Matthew 4:7 Deut. 6:16

Matthew 4:10 Deut. 6:13

CHAPTER 20
JESUS THE REDEEMER

Who forgiveth all thine iniquities; who healeth all thy diseases. (Psalms 103:3 KJV)

Scripture in both the Old and New Testaments revealed God's plan to break the power of iniquity. God would send his son who did not sin, transgress, rebel, or have an iniquity problem to pay the penalty for those who did (Isaiah 7;14, Luke 1:26-35).

> For he hath made him [to be] sin for us, who knew no sin; that we might be made the righteousness of God in him. (2 Corinthians 5:21 KJV)

Isaiah the prophet lived approximately 700 years prior to Jesus dying on the cross. His prophecy provides tremendous details of how Jesus would suffer by his sacrificial death for our sins.

> 3He was despised and rejected by mankind, a man of suffering, and familiar with pain. Like one from whom people hide their faces he was despised, and we held him in low esteem.4 Surely he took up our pain and bore our suffering, yet we considered him punished by God, stricken by him, and afflicted. 5 But he was pierced for our transgressions, he was crushed for our iniquities; the punishment that brought us peace was on him, and by his wounds we are healed.6 We all, like sheep, have gone astray, each of us has turned to our own way; and the LORD has laid on him the iniquity of us all. 7He was oppressed and afflicted, yet he did not open his mouth; he was led like a lamb to the slaughter, and as a sheep before its shearer is silent, so he did not open his mouth.8 By oppression and judgment he was taken away. Yet who of his generation protested? For he was cut off from the land of the living; for the transgression of my people, he was punished. After he has suffered, he will see the light of life and be satisfied; by his knowledge my righteous servant will justify many, and he will bear their iniquities. Isaiah 53:3-8,11 NIV)

Jesus paid iniquity's penalty and the guilt that came with it (Isaiah 53:6). "Jesus himself became our guilt offering." (Isaiah 53:12 CSB) The iniquity of every one of us fell upon on a man who never ever sinned. Think about it.

Astray "ta`ah" in Isaiah 53:6 (Strong's H8582) means "to vacillate, (cause to) go astray, deceive, dissemble, err, pant, seduce, (make to) stagger, (cause to) wander."[1] This definition contains some reasons why we like sheep may stray. It comes by some form of deception. Eve went astray once Satan's deceptive words stirred up lust which led her to sin. Adam just rebelled, which of course happens to be an easy route to iniquity (1 Tim 2:14). Scripture's first mention of Satan's interaction with humans came from the form of a serpent. This serpent's "crafty" description reveals his deceitful ways from the onset with man (Genesis 3:1).

Isaiah 53:11 says, "For he shall bear their iniquities." Bear (Strong's H5445) "cabal" means "to carry a heavy burden; also, to receive the penalties which another has deserved" (Isaiah 53:4;11).[2] "Jesus carried our heavy burdens from our sins and became the recipient of every penalty our iniquities deserved.

The Book of Titus from the New Testament declares the same truth as Isaiah. Jesus redeemed mankind from all iniquity.

> Jesus gave himself for us, that he might redeem us from all iniquity, and purify unto himself a peculiar people, zealous of good works. (Titus 2:14 KJV)

In Titus 2:14 redeem "lytroo" (Strong's G3084) is defined as, "liberate by payment of ransom" or "to release on receipt of ransom.".[3] Purify "katharízō" (Strong's G2513) denotes "to cleanse, purge, purify."[4]

We are redeemed, cleansed, purged, and purified from all sin and iniquity. This takes place the very moment Jesus Christ becomes our Lord and Savior at new birth (John 3:15-16; Romans 10:9-10). Right then all the penalties of sin set against us were "paid in full." He purified and made us clean, which set us apart for his purposes. Jesus became the ransom payment which freed us from sin and iniquities' bondage.

> 10 And by that will, we have been made holy through the sacrifice of the body of Jesus Christ once for all. 14 For by one sacrifice he has made perfect forever those who are being made holy. (Hebrews 10:10;14 NIV) And their sins and iniquities will I remember no more. (Heb 10:17 KJV)

Footnotes

[1] "H8582 - ta`ah - Strong's Hebrew Lexicon (KJV)." Blue Letter Bible. Web. 22 Apr 2020.

[2] "H5445 - cabal - Strong's Hebrew Lexicon (KJV)." Blue Letter Bible. Web. 11 May 2020.

[3] "G3084 - lytroō - Strong's Greek Lexicon (KJV)." Blue Letter Bible. Web. 16 May 2020.

[4] "G2511 - katharizō - Strong's Greek Lexicon (KJV)." Blue Letter Bible. Web. 16 May 2020.

Chapter 21
Blood and Atonement

The first mention of blood in scripture occurred when Cain killed his brother. Abel's blood cried out to God.

> 8 Now Cain said to his brother Abel, "Let's go out to the field." While they were in the field, Cain attacked his brother Abel and killed him. 9 Then the LORD said to Cain, "Where is your brother Abel?" "I don't know," he replied. "Am I my brother's keeper?" 10 The LORD said, "What have you done? Listen! Your brother's blood cries out to me from the ground." (Genesis 4:8-10 NIV).

The King James Bible states, "The voice of thy brother's blood crieth unto me from the ground. (Genesis 4:10 KJV). A Biblical truth we discover here: innocent blood shed by another has a voice, and it cries out to God. In Genesis 4:8-10, "voice" (Strong's H6963) means "to call aloud" and "blood (Strong's H1818) that when shed causes death."[12] 1, 2

This same truth comes from those martyred in the Book of Revelations 6:9-11. "And they cried with a loud voice, saying, 'How long, O Lord, holy and true, dost thou not judge and avenge our blood on them that dwell on the earth?'" (Revelation 6:10 NIV) They sought God to "judge and avenge" their blood (Revelations 6:10).

Leviticus 17:11 contains another truth about blood. Life of a living creature is in the blood.

> For the life of a creature is in the blood, and I have given it to you to make atonement for yourselves on the altar; it is the blood that makes atonement for one's life. (Leviticus 17:11 NIV)

Atonement in Leviticus 17:11 means "to cover." 3 In fact, the law required "that nearly everything be cleansed with blood, and without the shedding of blood there is no forgiveness." (Hebrews 9:22 NIV)

God first used the blood of an animal in Genesis to atone for the sin of Adam and Eve. In Genesis 3:21, "The Lord God made garments of skin for Adam and his wife and clothed them" (NIV). The hide of the animal covered their physical body, and its blood provided the means for atonement for their sin.

In Exodus chapter 12, the Passover lamb reveals the power of atoning blood. The blood of a spotless, unblemished lamb stopped death's destruction for those who applied its blood. Blood placed on the door posts of a house covered the sins of those inside.

> 7 Then they are to take some of the blood and put it on the sides and tops of the doorframes of the houses where they eat the lambs. (Exodus 12:7)

Death struck in Egypt where the blood was not present but passed over those under the protective covering of the blood (Exodus 12:3-13). God revealed what it would take to cleanse mankind of sin. The blood of the unblemished lamb atones for the guilty. Animal blood could not do permanently what the blood of lamb of God (Jesus) accomplished on our behalf.

> 24 to Jesus the mediator of a new covenant, and to the sprinkled blood that speaks a better word than the blood of Abel. (Hebrews 12:24 NIV)

Footnotes

[1] "H6963 - qowl - Strong's Hebrew Lexicon (KJV)." Blue Letter Bible. Web. 16 May 2020.

[2] "H1818 - dam - Strong's Hebrew Lexicon (KJV)." Blue Letter Bible. Web. 6 May 2020.

Chapter 22
The Blood of Jesus

What did Jesus possess that no one else did? Untainted, sinless blood of the son of God. His blood was the only blood that could be used to cleanse people completely. The blood of Jesus doesn't just appease, it cleanses and frees from the guilt of iniquity and sin.

> And from Jesus Christ, [who is] the faithful witness, [and] the first begotten of the dead, and the prince of the kings of the earth. Unto him that loved us and washed us from our sins in his own blood. (Revelations 1:5 KJV)

God spoke in the Old Testament Book of Joel that "he would cleanse the blood of those not yet cleansed" (Joel 3:21).

> For I will cleanse their blood [that] I have not cleansed: for the LORD dwelleth in Zion. (Joel 3:21 KJV)

"Cleanse their blood" 'naqah' (Strong's H5352) denotes "to be empty, be clear, be pure, be free from guilt, be innocent."[1] What a powerful truth. Our blood can be cleansed by his blood. What can be carried in a bloodline? Iniquity and guilt from the previous generations.

Animal blood was used temporarily under the Old Covenant to atone for sin. This ended in the New Covenant which required the sinless lamb of God to offer his blood once and for all.

> 12 he entered the most holy place once for all time, not by the blood of goats and calves, but by his own blood, having obtained eternal redemption. 13 For if the blood of goats and bulls and the ashes of a young cow, sprinkling those who are defiled, sanctify for the purification of the flesh, 14 how much more will the blood of Christ, who through the eternal Spirit offered himself without blemish to God, cleanse our consciences from dead works so that we can serve the living God? 15 Therefore, he is the mediator of a new covenant, so that those who are called might receive the promise of the eternal inheritance, because a death has taken place for redemption from the transgressions committed under the first covenant. (Hebrews 9:12-15 CSB)

Not only are we cleaned by the blood of Jesus, our conscience, receives the same benefit. Freedom from guilt became possible.

> Therefore, since we have now been justified [declared free of the guilt of sin] by His blood, [how much more certain is it that] we will be saved from the wrath of God through Him. Roman's 5:9 AMP

Without the blood of Jesus, there would be no triumph over sin and no stopping iniquity. As Jesus hung on that cross, the full magnitude of sin fell upon him.

"Jesus cried out, My God, My God, why have You forsaken Me?" (Matthew 27:46)

At that point Jesus became "totally abandoned, utterly forsaken" by God. I believe Jesus was crying out to God the Father and God the Holy Spirit. Jesus himself, God, the word had never been separated from the Father nor the Holy Spirit.

From the beginning in Genesis chapter 1, the Father, the Son (Word who became flesh), and the Spirit (Holy Spirit) appeared together. God is one in three persons (Genesis 1:1-3). It took God himself to die in our place as payment for every penalty set against us. Jesus experienced total separation from the love of his Father and the Presence of the Holy Spirit.

He was delivered over to death for our sins and was raised to life for our justification. (Romans 4:25 NIV)

Justification "(Strongs G1347)" dikaiosis means "the act of God declaring men free from guilt and acceptable to him."[2] Such love displayed by Jesus on the cross. Let us never forget the power of the blood of Jesus and his horrific suffering that set us free.

Footnotes

[1] "H5352"- naqah - Strong's Hebrew Lexicon (KJV)." Blue Letter Bible. Web. 6 May 2020.

[2] "G1347"- dikaiosis - Strong's Greek Lexicon (KJV)." Blue Letter Bible. Web. 3 June 2020.

CHAPTER 23
AUTHORITY OF THE NAME OF JESUS

In dealing with iniquity, one will need to use the name of Jesus and the authority it carries.

> Therefore, God exalted him to the highest place and gave him the name that is above every name, that at the name of Jesus every knee should bow, in heaven and on earth and under the earth. (Philippians 2:9-10 NIV)

God gave Jesus the name that is over every other name (Philippians 2:9-10). When iniquity visits, you may become aware of the presence of temptation. It could be incited by a demonic spirit. This becomes the occasion to use the authority of the name of Jesus. Ephesians 1:19-22 provides a good description of the authority of Jesus, and the authority his name contains for the believer.

> 19 ... and his incomparably great power for us who believe. That power is the same as the mighty strength 20 he exerted when he raised Christ from the dead and seated him at his right hand in the heavenly realms, 21 far above all rule and authority, power and dominion, and every name that is invoked, not only in the present age but also in the one to come. 22 And God placed all things under his feet and appointed him to be head over everything for the church. (Ephesians 1:19-22)

As Jesus fulfilled his earthly ministry, people were surprised at the authority and power he demonstrated over evil spirits.

> All the people were amazed and said to each other, "What words these are! With authority and power, he gives orders to impure spirits and they come out!" (Luke 4:36)

"In the synagogue there was a man possessed by a demon, an impure spirit. He cried out at the top of his voice, 34 Go away! What do you want with us, Jesus of Nazareth? Have you come to destroy us? I know who you are—the Holy One of God!"35 "Be quiet!" Jesus said sternly. "Come out of him!" Then the demon threw the man down before them all and came out without injuring him (Luke 4:33-36). This scripture demonstrates Jesus and his authority over demonic spirits.

In the book of Luke, Jesus sent seventy-two of his disciples out with his authority to do the very same thing as he did.

> "17 The seventy-two returned with joy and said, "Lord, even the demons submit to us in your name." 18 He replied, "I saw Satan fall like lightning from heaven. 19 I have given you authority to trample on snakes and scorpions and to overcome all the power of the enemy; nothing will harm you. 20 However, do not rejoice that the spirits submit to you, but rejoice that your names are written in heaven." (Luke 10:17-20)

Then Jesus came to them and said, "All authority in heaven and on earth has been given to me." (Matthew 28:18 NIV)

This same authority of Jesus belongs to believers in our day and hour too. When a spirit throws fiery darts (thoughts) your way, it may seek to lure you into a trap of iniquity. It could be a temptation that someone in one's your family line did not resist. Or it can be a new temptation of the enemy. Once you become aware of the tempting thoughts, reject them. Then in the authority and the name of Jesus, tell it to go. Next, quote the word of God that counters that temptation.

For example, if temped by the sin of pride, once recognized, go to the Lord and ask him to search your heart for any pride." If pride exists, then humble oneself before the Lord. Repent and ask him to forgive you of the sin of pride. Then in the Name of Jesus, command the "spirit of pride" to go. Next, quote the word (scripture) than counters the temptation. Such as, "My sacrifice is a humble spirit, O God; you will not reject a humble and repentant heart." (Psalm 51:17 Good News Translation) Then declare, "I have a humble and repentant heart." This counters the spirit of pride. Be aware that when Jesus was tempted, Satan left him but planned to return.

> "When the devil had finished all this tempting, he left him until an opportune time." (Luke 4:13 NIV)

Chapter 24
Nephilim in the Blood Line

And because iniquity shall abound, the love of many shall wax cold. Matthew 24:12 (KJV)

We previously covered iniquity's origins, which began with Lucifer. His iniquity (guilt) transferred to Adam and Eve. When this first couple disobeyed God and obeyed Satan, they received Satan's fallen, spirit nature. From them, Satan's iniquity transferred death to the spirits of all men. Physical death came upon the flesh of man as well. God created humans a triune being with a spirit, soul, and body (1 Thessalonians 5:23). Human life as God designed changed drastically. Men no longer set their hearts on a union with God.

Then Satan sought to move through the bloodline of mankind to secure earth as his own. Recall "life of the flesh is in the blood" (Leviticus 17:11). If Satan could thoroughly taint the blood of man, he could achieve his goal of god over earth. Earth would be transformed totally to evil. It would be hell on earth.

From the Book of Matthew, chapter one, a genealogy of the bloodline of Jesus can be found. It shows how God maneuvered from the bloodline of Abraham, thru King David to produce Mary and Joseph. From this bloodline, God chose Joseph to raise and influence Jesus as an earthly father. God did not go through Cain's bloodlines, but Seth's to produce Jesus. Cain's murder of Abel provided a lineage for Satan's use to pollute the bloodline of man. Jesus could not come from that bloodline. In the genealogy of Cain, the bloodline and the sins of the Nephilim emerged. God needed to keep a blood route to produce Jesus without Nephilim blood.

In the Nephilim there exists a heart problem. I'm not talking about a physical heart. There are those who go through the motions, but a disconnect exists between their hearts and emotions. Jesus required a close, Spirit to Spirit love connection with the Father and the Holy Spirit. It is dangerous to go through religious motions without a heart-to-heart love connection with God. Thank God, Jesus provided a bloodline that connects us purely and completely back to our Heavenly Father.

Next, Satan's plan to seize mankind occurred when fallen angels' lust after the daughters of men (Genesis 6). Angels were not created with physical bodies since they are celestial beings. However, angels can appear in the form of men. These fallen angels bred with women. What did Satan do with this? He introduced a corruption into the genetics and the bloodline of men. God already declared this would happen. There would be a war on earth with the seed of the devil and those of God (Genesis 3:15).

These fallen angels were in rebellion not only to God, but they also polluted the bloodline of men. The Nephilim bloodline introduced a double whammy against men. People who lack conscious. These people are brute beasts. They go through the motions, but their hearts are far from God. They are religious without relationship with Jesus. They seize weak willed people into their trap.

Satan thought he had completely done what he needed to take over. Nonetheless, the blood and the body of Jesus triumphantly defeated him. Now we walk on earth with the seed of man and the devil's seed.

> And I will put enmity between thee and the woman, and between thy seed and her seed; it shall bruise thy head, and thou shalt bruise his heel. (Genesis 3:15 KJV)

The infiltration of these types of people into the church, produces religious activity without relationship with God. This is a far cry from the Bride of Christ who makes herself ready (Rev 19:7-8). For further study on the Nephilim, get my book, *Living with the Nephilim, the Seed of Destruction* by V. Bryan.

Chapter 25
Judgement on Earth

"And they shall come back here in the fourth generation, for the iniquity of the Amorites is not yet complete." (Genesis 15:16 ESV)

At a time when Abraham remained childless, the Lord spoke of his descendants to come. "Know certainly that your descendants will be strangers in a land [that is] not theirs, and will serve them, and they will afflict them four hundred years (Genesis 15:13 NKJV). "¹⁶ But in the fourth generation they shall come hither again: for the iniquity of the Amorites is not yet full." (Genesis 15:16 (KJV)

In Genesis 15:16, the term "iniquity" is mentioned for the first time in the Bible. Here the generational problem of iniquity becomes exposed, which impacts both people and their land.

> And the land is defiled: therefore, I do visit the iniquity thereof upon it, and the land itself vomiteth out her inhabitants. (Leviticus 18:25 KJV)

Iniquity in Genesis 15:16 is avon again. The Amorites "depraved actions" did not warrant their destruction until the fourth generation. This reveals that the flow of iniquity in an entire people group can remain constant through four generations. (Exodus 34:7) Amorites were the descendants of Ham through Canaan (Genesis 10:15-16).

Iniquity permeates a land and its people just as with the Amorites. People keep falling into the iniquity trap as they join the guilt of the previous generation by doing the same things.

Recall that the first definition of avon meant perversity. Perversity in the Amorite family line can be traced all the way back to Ham. Ham looked upon his father's nakedness (Genesis 9:22). That act opened the door to iniquity.

For a more thorough study on the descendants of Ham, please get a copy of my book *Living with Nephilim the Seed of Destruction*. In my book *Origins of a Psychopath*, I went through the iniquity which operated in the family line of Adolf Hitler. To find out more about Hitler's family line, get a copy of that book. It is highly interesting and worth the read.

Canaanite territory likewise included Sodom and Gomorrah. (Genesis 10:18-19) In the Book of Genesis, God sent two angels to Sodom and Gomorrah to destroy these cities. Iniquity which flowed in this family line had gotten God's attention. An outcry reached heaven against them. (Genesis 18-19)

> ¹² The two men said to Lot, "Do you have anyone else here—sons-in-law, sons or daughters, or anyone else in the city who belongs to you? Get them out of here, 13 because we are going to

destroy this place. The outcry to the Lord against its people is so great that he has sent us to destroy it." Genesis 18:20

These angels warned Lot and his family to hurry and leave the cities. Iniquity of Sodom and Gomorrah warranted its destruction due to the grievous sins of its people.

> 15 And when the morning arose, then the angels hastened Lot, saying, Arise, take thy wife, and thy two daughters, which are here; lest thou be consumed in the iniquity of the city. Genesis 19:15 KJV

Iniquity in Genesis 19:15 is avon yet again. As with the Amorites, Sodom and Gomorrah's iniquity became full.

Not just a city or nation, but the entire earth comes under a curse due to the sins of its inhabitants.

Isaiah prophesied, "people must bear their guilt" (Isaiah 24:6).

> "³ The earth will be completely laid waste and totally plundered. The Lord has spoken this word. ⁴ The earth dries up and withers, the world languishes and withers, the heavens languish with the earth. ⁵ The earth is defiled by its people; they have disobeyed the laws, violated the statutes and broken the everlasting covenant. ⁶ Therefore a curse consumes the earth; its people must bear their guilt. Isaiah 24:3-6

In the Book of Genesis, Chapter 6, judgement of the entire earth occurred due to wickedness of the human race. "The Nephilim were on the earth in those days—and also afterward," which has a lot to do with the permeation of wickedness upon the earth. (Genesis 6)

> ¹¹ Now the earth was corrupt in God's sight and was full of violence. ¹² God saw how corrupt the earth had become, for all the people on earth had corrupted their ways. ¹³ So God said to Noah, "I am going to put an end to all people, for the earth is filled with violence because of them. I am surely going to destroy both them and the earth. Genesis 6:11-13

People, living creatures, along with the earth were destroyed by the flood. Only Noah and his family remained alive. (Genesis 6:8-10)

Corruption and violence describe the people on earth before the flood. It additionally describes Lucifer's iniquity as written in the Book of Ezekiel, chapter 28. Recall these scriptures below.

> Your heart became proud on account of your beauty, and you *corrupted* your wisdom because of your splendor. Ezekiel 28:17

> Through your widespread trade you were filled with *violence*, and you sinned. Ezekiel 28:16

"Corrupt" in Genesis 6:12-13 and "corrupted" in Ezekiel 28:17 happens to be the same word, Strong's H7843, "to destroy, corrupt, go to ruin, decay."[1] Violence, in Ezekiel 28:16 and Genesis 6:11,12, turns out to be the same word too, Strong's H2555. It means, "violence, wrong, oppression.[2]

Satan's iniquity did not have a problem transferring throughout earth. Iniquity still manifests with the same behaviors.

> ²⁶ "Just as it was in the days of Noah, so also will it be in the days of the Son of Man. ²⁷ People were eating, drinking, marrying and being given in marriage up to the day Noah entered the ark. Then the flood came and destroyed them all. ²⁸ "It was the same in the days of Lot. People were eating and drinking, buying and selling, planting and building. ²⁹ But the day Lot left Sodom, fire and sulfur rained down from heaven and destroyed them all. ³⁰ "It will be just like this on the day the Son of Man is revealed. Luke 17:26-30 NIV

In our day, the earth is full of corruption and violence just as well, we know this is so.

Do not ignore the signs of the times as they did in the days of Noah.

Footnotes

[1] "H7843 - šāḥaṯ - Strong's Hebrew Lexicon (kjv)." Blue Letter Bible. Web. 4 Jan, 2023.

[2] "H2555 - ḥāmās - Strong's Hebrew Lexicon (kjv)." Blue Letter Bible. Web. 4 Jan, 2023.

CHAPTER 26
GENEALOGY OF HEAVEN OR EARTH

Genesis chapter one supplies an overview of creation: the heavens, earth, and everything therein. Moses wrote Genesis chapter two with a different emphasis than the first chapter of Genesis. Genesis chapter one ends on day six, which happens to be the Biblical number for man.

> 1 Thus the heavens and the earth were completed, and all their hosts. 2 By the seventh day God completed His work which He had done, and He rested on the seventh day from all His work which He had done. 3 Then God blessed the seventh day and sanctified it, because in it He rested from all His work which God had created and made. (Genesis 2:1-3 NASB)

The work of God dealing with man spans to day seven of creation. A day in our understanding is a twenty-four-hour period, but we also recognize it is a division of time. We do not know how long a "day", or this separation of time may be in Genesis chapter two.[1]

> But do not let this one fact escape your notice, beloved, that with the Lord one day is like a thousand years, and a thousand years like one day. (2 Peter 3:8 NASB)

In Genesis 2:1, the work of day six was finished and by the seventh day (the Biblical number for God), "He rested from all his work which God had created and made." His work of creation was done. Interestingly, "the number seven also indicates spiritual perfection (Genesis 2:3).[2] Furthermore, on day seven when God's work was completed, the armies of heaven finally rested from war (Genesis 2:1-3).[3] We understand this by tsaba, the Hebrew word for host, which means "that which goes forth, army, war, warfare."[4] The armies of heaven cannot rest from warfare against Satan and his forces just yet. Just watch the news to understand our world fails greatly at perfection. In our day, war plays out for the souls of humanity on earth.

Next, in Genesis 2:4, Moses tells us about the generations of man.

> 4These are the generations of the heavens and of the earth when they were created, in the day that the LORD God made the earth and the heavens (Genesis 2:4 KJV).

Towlĕdah, the Hebrew word for generations, references "an account of men and their descendants, which is also a genealogical list."[5] Moses wanted us to know there are generations of heaven and generations of earth, and that they are different from one another. A person will be among those of heaven or of the earth and those who perish with it (Luke 10:20).

"The man" Adam was created eternal until he broke the command of God and sinned. At that point, he died spiritually, but his body lived on. This Hebrew word for lived, chayay, in Genesis 5:5 does means to "remain alive," which Adam did until his physical death.[6]

And all the days that Adam lived were nine hundred and thirty years: and he died. (Genesis 5:5 KJV)

Genesis chapter five lists the genealogy of Adam which began with his son Seth. Adam repented and was restored back to his relationship with God. Seth, like his dad, can be found listed in the genealogy of heaven. When Cain murdered his brother Abel, he left the presence of God. Cain became the first patriarch listed in the genealogy of earth. Moses does not list Cain or his lineage with Adam's descendants.

Footnotes

[1] Blue Letter Bible. "Dictionary and Word Search for yowm (Strong's 3117)". Blue Letter Bible. 2020.

[2] E. W. Bullinger. "The Meaning of Numbers in the Bible." Mar 26, 2012.

[3] Ibid.

[4] Blue Letter Bible. "Dictionary and Word Search for tsaba' (Strong's 6635)". Blue Letter Bible.

[5] Blue Letter Bible. "Dictionary and Word Search for towlĕdah (Strong's 8435)". Blue Letter Bible.

[6] Blue Letter Bible. "Dictionary and Word Search for (Strongs 2425)". Blue Letter Bible. Apr 1, 2012.

Chapter 27
Who's Your Daddy?

> 9 By this the love of God was manifested in us that God has sent His only begotten Son into the world so that we might live through Him. 10 In this is love, not that we loved God, but that He loved us and sent His Son to be the propitiation for our sins. (1 John 4:9-10 NASB)

All of us are born into Adam's sin and have personally done deeds to our own shame and condemnation. God, our Heavenly Father, made a way for all humankind to be restored back to His family and in His mercy. He sent a second Adam, Jesus Christ, who did not fail when Satan tempted him (Matthew 4:1-12).

> For there is one God, and one mediator also between God and men, the man Christ Jesus . . . (1 Timothy 2:5 NASB)

> And there is salvation in no one else; for there is no other name under heaven that has been given among men by which we must be saved. (Acts 4:12 NASB)

We must first truly repent for our sins. Jesus, both God and man, born of a virgin by the power of the Holy Spirit, never sinned. He had to live without sin to become the perfect sacrifice. Jesus bore the penalty for the sins of all humanity when He died on a cross. The blood of the innocent was shed for the guilty. Buried and three days later, by the power of God, His body came back to life. He returned to heaven and sits by the right hand of God, the Father always interceding for us (Matthew 1:18-25, I Peter 2:24, Acts 10:38-43).

> 8 But what does it say? "THE WORD IS NEAR YOU, IN YOUR MOUTH AND IN YOUR HEART"—that is, the word of faith which we are preaching, 9 that if you confess with your mouth Jesus as Lord, and believe in your heart that God raised Him from the dead, you will be saved; 10 for with the heart a person believes, resulting in righteousness, and with the mouth he confesses, resulting in salvation. (Romans 10:8-10 NASB)

If an individual has never asked Jesus to be his/her personal Lord and Savior, then what He did on the cross does not apply to them. Without Jesus, a person would pay the penalty for one's own sins and iniquity. The individual will be listed with the generations of the earth, separated from the Heavenly Father. Upon death, hell would be the sinner's punishment and final destination with the father of all sinners, Satan. "Jesus will say, 'I tell you I do not know you, where you are from. Depart from Me, all you workers of iniquity'" (Luke 13:27 NKJV)

Jesus said, "In my Father's house there are many rooms, and I will go and prepare a place for you (John 14:2)." If you have not repented of your sins, Satan will have successfully kept your soul for eternal punishment and away from a room in our Heavenly Father's house (Matthew 25:31-46).

If you would like to enter into a relationship with the Heavenly Father, it is time to pray.

Heavenly Father, I recognize I am a sinner. Please forgive me for all my wrongdoing. I am sorry and I want Jesus to save me. Lord Jesus, you bore all sin and the punishment I deserve on the cross. I ask you to make me clean by your blood shed on the cross. Come into my heart and be my Lord and Savior. I choose to simply believe your word. I thank you because I ask; you answer this prayer and take me out of the Kingdom of Darkness and place me into the Kingdom of Light with Jesus.

If you have drifted away from the Lord and would like to repent and come back, pray the above prayer, and mean it.

After all is said and done, eternity depends on the answer to one question: Who's your daddy? Two choices exist: the Heavenly Father, through faith in Jesus Christ, or Satan. May you choose correctly: it is a matter of eternal life or death.

> The LORD rewarded me according to my righteousness; according to the cleanness of my hands hath he recompensed me 21 For I have kept the ways of the LORD and have not wickedly departed from my God. (Psalm 18:20-21)

Iniquity Trap Workbook

Iniquity Chart

Iniquity in Your Family Line

Ever wonder what iniquities are at work in your own family line? You may discover this by filling out an iniquity chart. In these charts, you can go back three to four generations (Numbers 14:18, Exodus 34:7). Think about yourself and your parents, grandparents, great-grandparents and if possible, great-great grandparents. This would be difficult for me, I never met either of my grandfathers, nor do I know much about them.

Before beginning this process, I always suggest praying. Ask for God's guidance to reveal all that's at work within your family line. The Lord may bring back memories which will provide answers to this prayer. Think of areas of sin where your parent struggled. It might not seem like a major problem, but one that did affect them. Such an example could be addictive behavior such as with cigarettes and the like. Look for habits such as hoarding, overeating, multiple marriages, or unfaithfulness in relationships, etc. Additionally, look at the iniquity of your nationality. An example in this case would be Germans are known as quite avid beer drinkers. This could be a trait that plays into the iniquity of addiction such as alcoholism. Next think about the iniquity of your ethnic group. Do you see anything that stands out that operates in your life or family?

Stepparents who rear a child should be on the written section of the chart. Why? This person influences the children they raise. Joseph husband of Mary reared Jesus as his son. He knew Jesus's conception came by the Holy Spirit (Mathew 1:16; 18-25). Jesus was even listed in the lineage of Joseph back to King David and then to Abraham (Matthew 1:16). God chose Joseph and Mary to parent Jesus. Adopted children can fill out the chart with their adopted parents also. Concerning adopted children, I suggest you pray and ask the Lord what sins flow from their biological bloodline. Pay attention to the Holy Spirit for he will answer this prayer.

Additionally, think in terms of behavior, occupations, religious background, habits, vices, sin, and the like. Put these on the chart. Even think about diseases or sickness that appear in family lines. Add these where applicable. Then back up to your grandparents. Do the same with your mother's side of the family. Don't forget to look at aunts and uncles of your father and mother to identify iniquity patterns there too.

As the Iniquity Chart preparer, fill out a worksheet on yourself. What are the areas of sin you have personally experienced? Where do you struggle? What kind of things tempt you? What were the sin areas before you were born again? Do these areas still tempt you?

For example, if you were a biological child of King David, let's say Solomon, what would we know? He was tempted by the lust of the flesh with multiple sex partners at the same time. I would put down sexual lust (multiple sex partners).

Look at the sin areas of those on the chart. Look for twists and deviations of the same type of sin as seen in your father, grandfather, etc. Look at yourself and your siblings. Are there any similarities of sin? These same patterns of sin will seek the generations to come. Iniquity visits the next generation to set a trap. When finished with this chart, a greater awareness of the iniquity that lurks in your family line should emerge.

Victims of Iniquity

Have you been the victimized by another person? If so, what happened? Has this type of victimization occurred in your family line before? Add this information to the "Written Section" and the Iniquity Chart.

On the Positive Side

While filling out the chart, think about the good qualities, traits, abilities, and even gifting that exists among your family. Good attributes may pass on to the next generation too. Write these in as well. We know King David passed on iniquity to his family line, but he also passed on a heart after God. With Solomon in mind, he began his reign worshipping God faithfully as his father. Due to the iniquity trap, he did not end that way.

An example of good in my family would be from my dad. Along with being a good husband, father, and provider, he became an electrical engineer by profession. These positive abilities and traits passed onto his son and grandson. My dad also wrote a whole lot of correspondence, letters, and such. He kept great notes on everything he did. When I began to write books, I attribute this to a gifting that passed down from my dad.

At this point, I suggest you consider the positive attributes of those in your family. What are they? Write these on the written section of the chart. Honor them for the good they achieved.

COMPLETING THE CHART

The first step to completing your Iniquity Chart is to fill out "Iniquity Chart Worksheets. I refer to these as the "written section of the chart". Work sheets are provided to assist the gathering of information on at least three generations. Locate the worksheet that applies to you. For instance, the iniquity chart preparer is the person filling out the Iniquity Chart. This person represents a generation.

The chart preparer fills out the "Iniquity Chart Preparer's Worksheet (married or unmarried)". Next, find any other charts which applies, such as a chart on parents and grandparents. Then fill out as much as possible. There are also three charts for siblings available. One for the siblings of your father, mother, and the chart preparer. Siblings from the same family line can choose different iniquities. These sibling worksheets require only a brief overview. Write in any significant facts to aid iniquity's discovery.

The second step will be to fill out the Iniquity Chart Name References. This provides a quick name reference of those listed on your Iniquity Chart.

The third step will be to fill out the Iniquity Chart itself. Go through each column and place a check mark in the box that applies to any iniquity or disease relevant to that person. Space is provided to write in additional iniquity or diseases not listed. Each column represents one person. At the end of the chart, answer the overview questions. These questions highlight any discoveries from the Iniquity Chart. Don't forget to go to the end of the book, to the section on prayer.

Iniquity Trap Workbook

Written Section

INIQUITY CHART PREPARER WORKSHEET

My Immediate Family

Name

_____

Chart # _____

(Husband)

First Name _____ Last Name _____ Ethnic Group _____

    Birthplace _____ Birth date _____

    Marriage Date _____ Place of Marriage _____

    Health Issues _____ Wife(s) _____

    Occupation _____

Father's First and Last Name _____

Religious Affiliation _____

Overview of your Life: (Think in terms of behavior, occupations, divorce, vices, victimization, sin, and the like. Even think about diseases or sickness. Then add any other issues that needs to be noted.)

_____
_____
_____
_____
_____
_____
_____
_____
_____
_____
_____

On the Positive Side (Now think about good qualities, traits, abilities, and even gifting).
_____
_____
_____
_____
_____
_____

(Wife)

First Name _____ Last Name _____ Ethnic Group _____

    Birthplace_____ Birth date_____

    Marriage Date_____ Place of Marriage _____

    Health Issues_____ Wife(s) _____

    Occupation_____

Father's First and Last Name _____

Religious Affiliation _____

Overview of your Life: (Think in terms of behavior, occupations, divorce, vices, victimization, sin, and the like. Even think about diseases or sickness. Then add any other issues that needs to be noted.)

_____
_____
_____
_____
_____
_____
_____
_____
_____
_____
_____
_____

On the Positive Side (Now think about good qualities, traits, abilities, and even gifting).

_____
_____
_____
_____
_____
_____
_____
_____

Children (Including any miscarriages, adopted, born outside of marriage or with another partner)

Name	Gender	Birth Date	Birthplace	Adopted	Father/Mother

INIQUITY CHART

Chart # _____

(Page 2)

INIQUITY CHART WORKSHEET
Unmarried Preparer

Name

_____

Chart # _____

My Immediate Family

First Name _____ Last Name _____ Ethnic Group _____

Birthplace _____ Birth date _____

Previous Marriage (s) _____

Health Issues _____ Occupation _____

Religious Affiliation _____

Overview of your Life: (Think in terms of behavior, occupations, divorce, vices, victimization, sin, and the like. Even think about diseases or sickness. Then add any other issues that needs to be noted.)

_____
_____
_____
_____
_____
_____
_____
_____
_____
_____
_____
_____
_____

On the Positive Side (Now think about good qualities, traits, abilities, and even gifting).

_____
_____
_____
_____
_____
_____
_____
_____
_____
_____

Children (Including any miscarriages, adopted, born outside of marriage or with another partner).

Name	Gender	Birth Date	Birthplace	Adopted	Father/Mother

INIQUITY CHART

Chart # _____

(Page 2)

Father's Side of Family

Worksheets

INIQUITY CHART FAMILY WORKSHEET

Father and Mother

Chart # _____

Father (Husband)

First Name _____ Last Name _____ Ethnic Group _____

Birthplace _____ Birth date _____

Marriage Date _____ Place of Marriage _____

Date of Death _____ Place of Death _____

Cause of Death _____

Health _____ Other Wives _____

Occupation _____

Father's First and Last Name _____

Religious Affiliation _____

Overview of your Life: (Think in terms of behavior, occupations, divorce, vices, victimization, sin, and the like. Even think about diseases or sickness. Then add any other issues that needs to be noted.)

_____
_____
_____
_____
_____
_____
_____
_____
_____

On the Positive Side (Now think about good qualities, traits, abilities, and even gifting).

_____
_____
_____
_____
_____
_____
_____
_____
_____

INIQUITY CHART

Chart # _____

(Page 2)

Mother (Wife)

First Name _____ Last Name _____ Ethnic Group _____

Birthplace _____ Birth date _____

Marriage Date _____ Place of Marriage _____

Date of Death _____ Place of Death _____

Cause of Death _____

Health _____ Other Husbands _____

Occupation _____

Father's First and Last Name _____

Religious Affiliation _____

Overview of your Life: (Think in terms of behavior, occupations, divorce, vices, victimization, sin, and the like. Even think about diseases or sickness. Then add any other issues that needs to be noted.)

_____
_____
_____
_____
_____
_____
_____
_____
_____
_____
_____
_____
_____
_____
_____
_____
_____

On the Positive Side (Now think about good qualities, traits, abilities, and even gifting).

_____
_____
_____
_____
_____
_____
_____
_____
_____
_____
_____
_____
_____
_____
_____
_____
_____

Children (Including any miscarriages, adopted, born outside of marriage or with another partner).

Name	Gender	Birth Date	Birthplace	Adopted	Father/Mother

INIQUITY CHART

Chart # _____

(Page 2)

INIQUITY CHART FAMILY WORKSHEET

Grand Father & Grand Mother

Chart # _____

Grand Father (Husband)

First Name _____ Last Name _____ Ethnic Group _____

Birthplace _____ Birth date _____

Marriage Date _____ Place of Marriage _____

Date of Death _____ Place of Death _____

Cause of Death _____

Health _____ Other Wives _____

Occupation _____

Father's First and Last Name _____

Religious Affiliation _____

Overview of your Life: (Think in terms of behavior, occupations, divorce, vices, victimization, sin, and the like. Even think about diseases or sickness. Then add any other issues that needs to be noted.)

_____
_____
_____
_____
_____
_____
_____
_____
_____
_____

On the Positive Side (Now think about good qualities, traits, abilities, and even gifting).
_____
_____
_____
_____
_____
_____
_____
_____
_____
_____

INIQUITY CHART

Chart # _____

(Page 2)

Grand Mother (Wife)

First Name _____ Last Name _____ Ethnic Group _____

    Birthplace_____ Birth date _____

    Marriage Date _____ Place of Marriage _____

    Date of Death _____ Place of Death _____

    Cause of Death _____

    Health _____ Other Husbands _____

    Occupation _____

    Father's First and Last Name _____

    Religious Affiliation _____

Overview of your Life: (Think in terms of behavior, occupations, divorce, vices, victimization, sin, and the like. Even think about diseases or sickness. Then add any other issues that needs to be noted.)

_____
_____
_____
_____
_____
_____
_____
_____
_____
_____
_____
_____
_____
_____
_____
_____

On the Positive Side (Now think about good qualities, traits, abilities, and even gifting).

_____
_____
_____
_____
_____
_____
_____
_____
_____
_____
_____
_____
_____
_____
_____
_____

Children (Including any miscarriages, adopted, born outside of marriage or with another partner).

Name	Gender	Birth Date	Birthplace	Adopted	Father/Mother

INIQUITY CHART

Chart # _____

(Page 2)

INIQUITY CHART FAMILY WORKSHEET

Great-Grand Father & Great-Grand Mother

Chart # _____

Great-Grand Father (Husband)

First Name _____ Last Name _____ Ethnic Group _____

Birthplace _____ Birth date _____

Marriage Date _____ Place of Marriage _____

Date of Death _____ Place of Death _____

Cause of Death _____

Health _____ Other Wives _____

Occupation _____

Father's First and Last Name _____

Religious Affiliation _____

Overview of your Life: (Think in terms of behavior, occupations, divorce, vices, victimization, sin, and the like. Even think about diseases or sickness. Then add any other issues that needs to be noted.)

_____
_____
_____
_____
_____
_____
_____
_____
_____
_____
_____

On the Positive Side (Now think about good qualities, traits, abilities, and even gifting).

_____
_____
_____
_____
_____
_____
_____
_____
_____
_____

INIQUITY CHART

Chart # _____

(Page 2)

Great-Grand Mother (Wife)

First Name _____ Last Name _____ Ethnic Group _____

Birthplace _____ Birth date _____

Marriage Date _____ Place of Marriage _____

Date of Death _____ Place of Death _____

Cause of Death _____

Health _____ Other Husbands _____

Occupation _____

Father's First and Last Name _____

Religious Affiliation _____

Overview of your Life: (Think in terms of behavior, occupations, divorce, vices, victimization, sin, and the like. Even think about diseases or sickness. Then add any other issues that needs to be noted.)

_____
_____
_____
_____
_____
_____
_____
_____
_____
_____
_____
_____
_____
_____
_____
_____

On the Positive Side (Now think about good qualities, traits, abilities, and even gifting).

_____
_____
_____
_____
_____
_____
_____
_____
_____
_____
_____
_____
_____
_____
_____
_____
_____

Children (Including any miscarriages, adopted, born outside of marriage or with another partner).

Name	Gender	Birth Date	Birthplace	Adopted	Father/Mother

INIQUITY CHART

Chart # _____

(Page 2)

INIQUITY CHART FAMILY WORKSHEET

Great-Great-Grand Father & Great-Great-Grand Mother

Chart # _____

Great-Great-Grand Father (Husband)

First Name _____ Last Name _____ Ethnic Group _____

Birthplace _____ Birth date _____

Marriage Date _____ Place of Marriage _____

Date of Death _____ Place of Death _____

Cause of Death _____

Health _____ Other Wives _____

Occupation _____

Father's First and Last Name _____

Religious Affiliation _____

Overview of your Life: (Think in terms of behavior, occupations, divorce, vices, victimization, sin, and the like. Even think about diseases or sickness. Then add any other issues that needs to be noted.)

_____
_____
_____
_____
_____
_____
_____
_____
_____
_____

On the Positive Side (Now think about good qualities, traits, abilities, and even gifting).

_____
_____
_____
_____
_____
_____
_____
_____
_____
_____

INIQUITY CHART

Chart # _____

(Page 2)

Great-Great-Grand Mother (Wife)

First Name _____ Last Name _____ Ethnic Group _____

    Birthplace _____ Birth date _____

    Marriage Date _____ Place of Marriage _____

    Date of Death _____ Place of Death _____

    Cause of Death _____

    Health _____ Other Husbands _____

    Occupation _____

    Father's First and Last Name _____

    Religious Affiliation _____

Overview of your Life: (Think in terms of behavior, occupations, divorce, vices, victimization, sin, and the like. Even think about diseases or sickness. Then add any other issues that needs to be noted.)

_____
_____
_____
_____
_____
_____
_____
_____
_____
_____
_____
_____
_____
_____
_____
_____

On the Positive Side (Now think about good qualities, traits, abilities, and even gifting).

_____
_____
_____
_____
_____
_____
_____
_____
_____
_____
_____
_____
_____
_____
_____
_____

Children (Including any miscarriages, adopted, born outside of marriage or with another partner).

Name	Gender	Birth Date	Birthplace	Adopted	Father/Mother

INIQUITY CHART

Chart # _____

(Page 2)

INIQUITY CHART ADOPTED FAMILY WORKSHEET

Chart # _____

Father by Adoption (Husband)

First Name _____ Last Name _____ Ethnic Group _____

    Birthplace _____ Birth date _____

    Marriage Date _____ Place of Marriage _____

    Date of Death _____ Place of Death _____

    Cause of Death _____

    Health _____ Other Wives _____

    Occupation _____

    Father's First and Last Name _____

    Religious Affiliation _____

Overview of your Life: (Think in terms of behavior, occupations, divorce, vices, victimization, sin, and the like. Even think about diseases or sickness. Then add any other issues that needs to be noted.)

_____
_____
_____
_____
_____
_____
_____
_____
_____
_____
_____

On the Positive Side (Now think about good qualities, traits, abilities, and even gifting).

_____
_____
_____
_____
_____
_____
_____
_____
_____
_____

INIQUITY CHART

Chart # _____

(Page 2)

Mother by Adoption (Wife)

First Name _____ Last Name _____ Ethnic Group _____

Birthplace _____ Birth date _____

Marriage Date _____ Place of Marriage _____

Date of Death _____ Place of Death _____

Cause of Death _____

Health _____ Other Husbands _____

Occupation _____

Father's First and Last Name _____

Religious Affiliation _____

Overview of your Life: (Think in terms of behavior, occupations, divorce, vices, victimization, sin, and the like. Even think about diseases or sickness. Then add any other issues that needs to be noted.)

_____
_____
_____
_____
_____
_____
_____
_____

On the Positive Side (Now think about good qualities, traits, abilities, and even gifting).

_____
_____
_____
_____
_____
_____
_____
_____

Story Behind Adoption:

_____
_____
_____
_____
_____
_____

Children (Including any other children, adopted or natural birth).

Name	Gender	Birth Date	Birthplace	Adopted	Father/Mother

INIQUITY CHART

Chart # _____

(Page 2)

Mother's Side of Family

Worksheets

INIQUITY CHART FAMILY WORKSHEET

Father and Mother

Chart # _____

Father (Husband)

First Name _____ Last Name _____ Ethnic Group _____

    Birthplace_____ Birth date _____

    Marriage Date _____ Place of Marriage _____

    Date of Death _____ Place of Death _____

    Cause of Death _____

    Health _____ Other Wives _____

    Occupation _____

    Father's First and Last Name _____

    Religious Affiliation _____

Overview of your Life: (Think in terms of behavior, occupations, divorce, vices, victimization, sin, and the like. Even think about diseases or sickness. Then add any other issues that needs to be noted.)

_____
_____
_____
_____
_____
_____
_____
_____
_____
_____

On the Positive Side (Now think about good qualities, traits, abilities, and even gifting).

_____
_____
_____
_____
_____
_____
_____
_____
_____
_____

INIQUITY CHART

Chart # _____

(Page 2)

Mother (Wife)

First Name _____ Last Name _____ Ethnic Group _____

Birthplace _____ Birth date _____

Marriage Date _____ Place of Marriage _____

Date of Death _____ Place of Death _____

Cause of Death _____

Health _____ Other Husbands _____

Occupation _____

Father's First and Last Name _____

Religious Affiliation _____

Overview of your Life: (Think in terms of behavior, occupations, divorce, vices, victimization, sin, and the like. Even think about diseases or sickness. Then add any other issues that needs to be noted.)

_____
_____
_____
_____
_____
_____
_____
_____
_____
_____
_____
_____
_____
_____
_____

On the Positive Side (Now think about good qualities, traits, abilities, and even gifting).

_____
_____
_____
_____
_____
_____
_____
_____
_____
_____
_____
_____
_____
_____
_____
_____

Children (Including any miscarriages, adopted, born outside of marriage or with another partner).

Name	Gender	Birth Date	Birthplace	Adopted	Father/Mother

INIQUITY CHART

Chart # _____

(Page 2)

INIQUITY CHART FAMILY WORKSHEET

Grand Father & Grand Mother

Chart # _____

Grand Father (Husband)

First Name _____ Last Name _____ Ethnic Group _____

Birthplace _____ Birth date _____

Marriage Date _____ Place of Marriage _____

Date of Death _____ Place of Death _____

Cause of Death _____

Health _____ Other Wives _____

Occupation _____

Father's First and Last Name _____

Religious Affiliation _____

Overview of your Life: (Think in terms of behavior, occupations, divorce, vices, victimization, sin, and the like. Even think about diseases or sickness. Then add any other issues that needs to be noted.)

_____
_____
_____
_____
_____
_____
_____
_____
_____
_____

On the Positive Side (Now think about good qualities, traits, abilities, and even gifting).

_____
_____
_____
_____
_____
_____
_____
_____
_____
_____

INIQUITY CHART

Chart # _____

(Page 2)

Grand Mother (Wife)

First Name _____ Last Name _____ Ethnic Group _____

Birthplace _____ Birth date _____

Marriage Date _____ Place of Marriage _____

Date of Death _____ Place of Death _____

Cause of Death _____

Health _____ Other Husbands _____

Occupation _____

Father's First and Last Name _____

Religious Affiliation _____

Overview of your Life: (Think in terms of behavior, occupations, divorce, vices, victimization, sin, and the like. Even think about diseases or sickness. Then add any other issues that needs to be noted.)

_____
_____
_____
_____
_____
_____
_____
_____
_____
_____
_____
_____
_____
_____
_____
_____

On the Positive Side (Now think about good qualities, traits, abilities, and even gifting).

_____
_____
_____
_____
_____
_____
_____
_____
_____
_____
_____
_____
_____
_____
_____
_____

Children (Including any miscarriages, adopted, born outside of marriage or with another partner).

Name	Gender	Birth Date	Birthplace	Adopted	Father/Mother

INIQUITY CHART

Chart # _____

(Page 2)

INIQUITY CHART FAMILY WORKSHEET

Great-Grand Father & Great-Grand Mother

Chart # _____

Great-Grand Father (Husband)

First Name _____ Last Name _____ Ethnic Group _____

Birthplace _____ Birth date _____

Marriage Date _____ Place of Marriage _____

Date of Death _____ Place of Death _____

Cause of Death _____

Health _____ Other Wives _____

Occupation _____

Father's First and Last Name _____

Religious Affiliation _____

Overview of your Life: (Think in terms of behavior, occupations, divorce, vices, victimization, sin, and the like. Even think about diseases or sickness. Then add any other issues that needs to be noted.)

_____
_____
_____
_____
_____
_____
_____
_____
_____
_____

On the Positive Side (Now think about good qualities, traits, abilities, and even gifting).

_____
_____
_____
_____
_____
_____
_____
_____
_____
_____

INIQUITY CHART

Chart # _____

(Page 2)

Great-Grand Mother (Wife)

First Name _____ Last Name _____ Ethnic Group _____

    Birthplace _____ Birth date _____

    Marriage Date _____ Place of Marriage _____

    Date of Death _____ Place of Death _____

    Cause of Death _____

    Health _____ Other Husbands _____

    Occupation _____

    Father's First and Last Name _____

    Religious Affiliation _____

Overview of your Life: (Think in terms of behavior, occupations, divorce, vices, victimization, sin, and the like. Even think about diseases or sickness. Then add any other issues that needs to be noted.)

_____
_____
_____
_____
_____
_____
_____
_____
_____
_____
_____
_____
_____
_____
_____
_____

On the Positive Side (Now think about good qualities, traits, abilities, and even gifting).

_____
_____
_____
_____
_____
_____
_____
_____
_____
_____
_____
_____
_____
_____
_____
_____
_____

Children (Including any miscarriages, adopted, born outside of marriage or with another partner).

Name	Gender	Birth Date	Birthplace	Adopted	Father/Mother

INIQUITY CHART

Chart # _____

(Page 2)

INIQUITY CHART FAMILY WORKSHEET

Great-Great-Grand Father & Great-Great-Grand Mother

Chart # _____

Great-Great-Grand Father (Husband)

First Name _____ Last Name _____ Ethnic Group _____

Birthplace _____ Birth date _____

Marriage Date _____ Place of Marriage _____

Date of Death _____ Place of Death _____

Cause of Death _____

Health _____ Other Wives _____

Occupation _____

Father's First and Last Name _____

Religious Affiliation _____

Overview of your Life: (Think in terms of behavior, occupations, divorce, vices, victimization, sin, and the like. Even think about diseases or sickness. Then add any other issues that needs to be noted.)

_____
_____
_____
_____
_____
_____
_____
_____
_____
_____

On the Positive Side (Now think about good qualities, traits, abilities, and even gifting).

_____
_____
_____
_____
_____
_____
_____
_____
_____
_____

INIQUITY CHART

Chart # _____

(Page 2)

Great-Great-Grand Mother (Wife)

First Name _____ Last Name _____ Ethnic Group _____

    Birthplace _____ Birth date _____

    Marriage Date _____ Place of Marriage _____

    Date of Death _____ Place of Death _____

    Cause of Death _____

    Health _____ Other Husbands _____

    Occupation _____

    Father's First and Last Name _____

    Religious Affiliation _____

Overview of your Life: (Think in terms of behavior, occupations, divorce, vices, victimization, sin, and the like. Even think about diseases or sickness. Then add any other issues that needs to be noted.)

_____
_____
_____
_____
_____
_____
_____
_____
_____
_____
_____
_____
_____
_____
_____
_____
_____

On the Positive Side (Now think about good qualities, traits, abilities, and even gifting).

_____
_____
_____
_____
_____
_____
_____
_____
_____
_____
_____
_____
_____
_____
_____
_____

Children (Including any miscarriages, adopted, born outside of marriage or with another partner).

Name	Gender	Birth Date	Birthplace	Adopted	Father/Mother

INIQUITY CHART

Chart # _____

(Page 2)

INIQUITY CHART ADOPTED FAMILY WORKSHEET

Chart # _____

Father by Adoption (Husband)

First Name _____ Last Name _____ Ethnic Group _____

Birthplace _____ Birth date _____

Marriage Date _____ Place of Marriage _____

Date of Death _____ Place of Death _____

Cause of Death _____

Health _____ Other Wives _____

Occupation _____

Father's First and Last Name _____

Religious Affiliation _____

Overview of your Life: (Think in terms of behavior, occupations, divorce, vices, victimization, sin, and the like. Even think about diseases or sickness. Then add any other issues that needs to be noted.)

_____
_____
_____
_____
_____
_____
_____
_____
_____
_____

On the Positive Side (Now think about good qualities, traits, abilities, and even gifting).

_____
_____
_____
_____
_____
_____
_____
_____
_____
_____

INIQUITY CHART

Chart # _____

(Page 2)

Mother by Adoption (Wife)

First Name _____ Last Name _____ Ethnic Group _____

Birthplace _____ Birth date _____

Marriage Date _____ Place of Marriage _____

Date of Death _____ Place of Death _____

Cause of Death _____

Health _____ Other Husbands _____

Occupation _____

Father's First and Last Name _____

Religious Affiliation _____

Overview of your Life: (Think in terms of behavior, occupations, divorce, vices, victimization, sin, and the like. Even think about diseases or sickness. Then add any other issues that needs to be noted.)

_____
_____
_____
_____
_____
_____
_____
_____

On the Positive Side (Now think about good qualities, traits, abilities, and even gifting).

_____
_____
_____
_____
_____
_____
_____

Story Behind Adoption:

_____
_____
_____
_____
_____
_____

Children (Including any other children, adopted or natural birth).

Name	Gender	Birth Date	Birthplace	Adopted	Father/Mother

INIQUITY CHART

Chart # _____

(Page 2)

MY FATHER'S SIBLINGS

(Your Aunts & Uncles)

Sb#1- name _____ Spouse _____
Overview _____

Sb#2- name _____ Spouse _____
Overview _____

Sb#3- name _____ Spouse _____
Overview _____

Sb#4- name _____ Spouse _____
Overview _____

Sb#5- name _____ Spouse _____
Overview _____

Sb#6- name _____ Spouse _____
Overview _____

Sb#7- name _____ Spouse _____
Overview _____

Sb#8- name _____ Spouse _____
Overview _____

Sb#9- name _____ Spouse _____
Overview _____

Sb#10- name _____ Spouse _____
Overview _____

INIQUITY CHART

Chart # _____

(Page 2)

MY MOTHER'S SIBLINGS
(Your Aunts & Uncles)

Sb#1- name _____ Spouse _____
Overview _____

Sb#2- name _____ Spouse _____
Overview _____

Sb#3- name _____ Spouse _____
Overview _____

Sb#4- name _____ Spouse _____
Overview _____

Sb#5- name _____ Spouse _____
Overview _____

Sb#6- name _____ Spouse _____
Overview _____

Sb#7- name _____ Spouse _____
Overview _____

Sb#8- name _____ Spouse _____
Overview _____

Sb#9- name _____ Spouse _____
Overview _____

Sb#10- name _____ Spouse _____
Overview _____

INIQUITY CHART

Chart # _____

(Page 2)

CHART PREPARER'S
Siblings

Sb#1- name _____ Spouse _____
Overview _____

Sb#2- name _____ Spouse _____
Overview _____

Sb#3- name _____ Spouse _____
Overview _____

Sb#4- name _____ Spouse _____
Overview _____

Sb#5- name _____ Spouse _____
Overview _____

Sb#6- name _____ Spouse _____
Overview _____

Sb#7- name _____ Spouse _____
Overview _____

Sb#8- name _____ Spouse _____
Overview _____

Sb#9- name _____ Spouse _____
Overview _____

Sb#10- name _____ Spouse _____
Overview _____

INIQUITY CHART

Chart # _____

(Page 2)

INIQUITY CHART

Name Reference

_____

Iniquity Chart Preparer

My Name

_____

Father's Side of the Family

Father _____

Father's Grandfather _____

Father's Great-Grandfather _____

Father's Grandmother _____

Father's Great-Grand Mother _____

Father's Wife _____

Mother Side of the Family

Mother's Father _____

Mother's Grandfather _____

Mother's Great-Grandfather _____

Mother's Mother _____

Mother's Grandmother _____

Mother's Great-Grandmother _____

Mother's Husband _____

My Father's Siblings
(Your Aunts & Uncles)

Sb#1-name _____

Sb#2-name _____

Sb#3-name _____

Sb#4-name _____

Sb#5-name _____

Sb#6-name _____

Sb#7-name _____

Sb#8-name _____

Sb#9-name _____

Sb#10-name _____

My Mother's Siblings
(Your Aunts & Uncles)

Sb#1-name _____

Sb#2-name _____

Sb#3-name _____

Sb#4-name _____

Sb#5-name _____

Sb#6-name _____

Sb#7-name _____

Sb#8-name _____

Sb#9-name _____

Sb#10-name _____

Chart Preparer's
Siblings

Sb#1-name _____

Sb#2-name _____

Sb#3-name _____

Sb#4-name _____

Sb#5-name _____

Sb#6-name _____

Sb#7-name _____

Sb#8-name _____

Sb#9-name _____

Sb#10-name _____

Iniquity Trap Chart

INIQUITY CHART

Instructions

Put an 'x' under the applicable iniquity of the family member listed.

Put an 'x' under the applicable disease or health problem of the family member listed.

Write in any iniquity or health issue not listed.

Quick Key

F	:	Father
M	:	Mother
ME	:	Chart Preparer
GF	:	Grandfather
GM	:	Grandmother
GGF	:	Great Grandfather
GGM	:	Great Grandmother

Father's Side

Iniquities	GGF	GF	F	ME	M	GM	GGM
Abortion	☐	☐	☐	☐	☐	☐	☐
Adultery	☐	☐	☐	☐	☐	☐	☐
Arrogance	☐	☐	☐	☐	☐	☐	☐
Boastful	☐	☐	☐	☐	☐	☐	☐
Child Abuse	☐	☐	☐	☐	☐	☐	☐
Criminal	☐	☐	☐	☐	☐	☐	☐
Divisive	☐	☐	☐	☐	☐	☐	☐
Envy	☐	☐	☐	☐	☐	☐	☐
Fornication	☐	☐	☐	☐	☐	☐	☐
God Hater	☐	☐	☐	☐	☐	☐	☐
Idolatry	☐	☐	☐	☐	☐	☐	☐
Lying	☐	☐	☐	☐	☐	☐	☐
Molestation	☐	☐	☐	☐	☐	☐	☐
Perfectionism	☐	☐	☐	☐	☐	☐	☐
Pride	☐	☐	☐	☐	☐	☐	☐
Rebellion	☐	☐	☐	☐	☐	☐	☐
Sexual Perversion	☐	☐	☐	☐	☐	☐	☐
Slander	☐	☐	☐	☐	☐	☐	☐
Suicide	☐	☐	☐	☐	☐	☐	☐
Unclean	☐	☐	☐	☐	☐	☐	☐
Witchcraft/Sorcery	☐	☐	☐	☐	☐	☐	☐
Abuse	☐	☐	☐	☐	☐	☐	☐
Alcoholic	☐	☐	☐	☐	☐	☐	☐
Bitterness	☐	☐	☐	☐	☐	☐	☐
Blood Shed	☐	☐	☐	☐	☐	☐	☐
Controlling	☐	☐	☐	☐	☐	☐	☐
Deceitful	☐	☐	☐	☐	☐	☐	☐
Divorce	☐	☐	☐	☐	☐	☐	☐
False Religion	☐	☐	☐	☐	☐	☐	☐
Gluttony	☐	☐	☐	☐	☐	☐	☐
Hatred	☐	☐	☐	☐	☐	☐	☐
Lack	☐	☐	☐	☐	☐	☐	☐

Iniquities	GGF	GF	F	ME	M	GM	GGM
Mammon	☐	☐	☐	☐	☐	☐	☐
Occult	☐	☐	☐	☐	☐	☐	☐
Pornography	☐	☐	☐	☐	☐	☐	☐
Prostitution	☐	☐	☐	☐	☐	☐	☐
Rejection	☐	☐	☐	☐	☐	☐	☐
Secrecy	☐	☐	☐	☐	☐	☐	☐
Stealing	☐	☐	☐	☐	☐	☐	☐
Unbelief	☐	☐	☐	☐	☐	☐	☐
Unforgiveness	☐	☐	☐	☐	☐	☐	☐
Addiction	☐	☐	☐	☐	☐	☐	☐
Anger/Rage	☐	☐	☐	☐	☐	☐	☐
Blasphemy	☐	☐	☐	☐	☐	☐	☐
Carousing	☐	☐	☐	☐	☐	☐	☐
Coveting	☐	☐	☐	☐	☐	☐	☐
Depression	☐	☐	☐	☐	☐	☐	☐
Drug Abuse	☐	☐	☐	☐	☐	☐	☐
Fearfulness	☐	☐	☐	☐	☐	☐	☐
Greed	☐	☐	☐	☐	☐	☐	☐
Hypocrite	☐	☐	☐	☐	☐	☐	☐
Lust	☐	☐	☐	☐	☐	☐	☐
Mental Illness	☐	☐	☐	☐	☐	☐	☐
Pride	☐	☐	☐	☐	☐	☐	☐
Poverty	☐	☐	☐	☐	☐	☐	☐
Quarreling	☐	☐	☐	☐	☐	☐	☐
Sexual Immorality	☐	☐	☐	☐	☐	☐	☐
Secret Society	☐	☐	☐	☐	☐	☐	☐
Strife	☐	☐	☐	☐	☐	☐	☐
Unwed Birth	☐	☐	☐	☐	☐	☐	☐
Violence	☐	☐	☐	☐	☐	☐	☐
	☐	☐	☐	☐	☐	☐	☐
	☐	☐	☐	☐	☐	☐	☐
	☐	☐	☐	☐	☐	☐	☐

Diseases/Illness	GGF	GF	F	ME	M	GM	GGM
Alzheimer's	☐	☐	☐	☐	☐	☐	☐
Childlessness	☐	☐	☐	☐	☐	☐	☐
Dementia	☐	☐	☐	☐	☐	☐	☐
Mental Illness	☐	☐	☐	☐	☐	☐	☐
Premature Death	☐	☐	☐	☐	☐	☐	☐
Arthritis	☐	☐	☐	☐	☐	☐	☐
Chronic Illness	☐	☐	☐	☐	☐	☐	☐
Heart disease	☐	☐	☐	☐	☐	☐	☐
Miscarriage	☐	☐	☐	☐	☐	☐	☐
Thyroid disorders	☐	☐	☐	☐	☐	☐	☐
Cancer	☐	☐	☐	☐	☐	☐	☐
Diabetes	☐	☐	☐	☐	☐	☐	☐
High blood pressure	☐	☐	☐	☐	☐	☐	☐
Multiple sclerosis	☐	☐	☐	☐	☐	☐	☐
	☐	☐	☐	☐	☐	☐	☐
	☐	☐	☐	☐	☐	☐	☐
Total Iniquities							
Total Diseases							

Father's Siblings

Iniquities	S1	S2	S3	S4	S5	S6	S7	S8	S9	S10
Abortion	☐	☐	☐	☐	☐	☐	☐	☐	☐	☐
Adultery	☐	☐	☐	☐	☐	☐	☐	☐	☐	☐
Arrogance	☐	☐	☐	☐	☐	☐	☐	☐	☐	☐
Boastful	☐	☐	☐	☐	☐	☐	☐	☐	☐	☐
Child Abuse	☐	☐	☐	☐	☐	☐	☐	☐	☐	☐
Criminal	☐	☐	☐	☐	☐	☐	☐	☐	☐	☐
Divisive	☐	☐	☐	☐	☐	☐	☐	☐	☐	☐
Envy	☐	☐	☐	☐	☐	☐	☐	☐	☐	☐
Fornication	☐	☐	☐	☐	☐	☐	☐	☐	☐	☐
God Hater	☐	☐	☐	☐	☐	☐	☐	☐	☐	☐
Idolatry	☐	☐	☐	☐	☐	☐	☐	☐	☐	☐
Lying	☐	☐	☐	☐	☐	☐	☐	☐	☐	☐
Molestation	☐	☐	☐	☐	☐	☐	☐	☐	☐	☐
Perfectionism	☐	☐	☐	☐	☐	☐	☐	☐	☐	☐
Pride	☐	☐	☐	☐	☐	☐	☐	☐	☐	☐
Rebellion	☐	☐	☐	☐	☐	☐	☐	☐	☐	☐
Sexual Perversion	☐	☐	☐	☐	☐	☐	☐	☐	☐	☐
Slander	☐	☐	☐	☐	☐	☐	☐	☐	☐	☐
Suicide	☐	☐	☐	☐	☐	☐	☐	☐	☐	☐
Unclean	☐	☐	☐	☐	☐	☐	☐	☐	☐	☐
Witchcraft/Sorcery	☐	☐	☐	☐	☐	☐	☐	☐	☐	☐
Abuse	☐	☐	☐	☐	☐	☐	☐	☐	☐	☐
Alcoholic	☐	☐	☐	☐	☐	☐	☐	☐	☐	☐
Bitterness	☐	☐	☐	☐	☐	☐	☐	☐	☐	☐
Blood Shed	☐	☐	☐	☐	☐	☐	☐	☐	☐	☐
Controlling	☐	☐	☐	☐	☐	☐	☐	☐	☐	☐
Deceitful	☐	☐	☐	☐	☐	☐	☐	☐	☐	☐
Divorce	☐	☐	☐	☐	☐	☐	☐	☐	☐	☐
False Religion	☐	☐	☐	☐	☐	☐	☐	☐	☐	☐
Gluttony	☐	☐	☐	☐	☐	☐	☐	☐	☐	☐
Hatred	☐	☐	☐	☐	☐	☐	☐	☐	☐	☐
Lack	☐	☐	☐	☐	☐	☐	☐	☐	☐	☐

Iniquities	S1	S2	S3	S4	S5	S6	S7	S8	S9	S10
Mammon	☐	☐	☐	☐	☐	☐	☐	☐	☐	☐
Occult	☐	☐	☐	☐	☐	☐	☐	☐	☐	☐
Pornography	☐	☐	☐	☐	☐	☐	☐	☐	☐	☐
Prostitution	☐	☐	☐	☐	☐	☐	☐	☐	☐	☐
Rejection	☐	☐	☐	☐	☐	☐	☐	☐	☐	☐
Secrecy	☐	☐	☐	☐	☐	☐	☐	☐	☐	☐
Stealing	☐	☐	☐	☐	☐	☐	☐	☐	☐	☐
Unbelief	☐	☐	☐	☐	☐	☐	☐	☐	☐	☐
Unforgiveness	☐	☐	☐	☐	☐	☐	☐	☐	☐	☐
Addiction	☐	☐	☐	☐	☐	☐	☐	☐	☐	☐
Anger/Rage	☐	☐	☐	☐	☐	☐	☐	☐	☐	☐
Blasphemy	☐	☐	☐	☐	☐	☐	☐	☐	☐	☐
Carousing	☐	☐	☐	☐	☐	☐	☐	☐	☐	☐
Coveting	☐	☐	☐	☐	☐	☐	☐	☐	☐	☐
Depression	☐	☐	☐	☐	☐	☐	☐	☐	☐	☐
Drug Abuse	☐	☐	☐	☐	☐	☐	☐	☐	☐	☐
Fearfulness	☐	☐	☐	☐	☐	☐	☐	☐	☐	☐
Greed	☐	☐	☐	☐	☐	☐	☐	☐	☐	☐
Hypocrite	☐	☐	☐	☐	☐	☐	☐	☐	☐	☐
Lust	☐	☐	☐	☐	☐	☐	☐	☐	☐	☐
Mental Illness	☐	☐	☐	☐	☐	☐	☐	☐	☐	☐
Pride	☐	☐	☐	☐	☐	☐	☐	☐	☐	☐
Poverty	☐	☐	☐	☐	☐	☐	☐	☐	☐	☐
Quarreling	☐	☐	☐	☐	☐	☐	☐	☐	☐	☐
Sexual Immorality	☐	☐	☐	☐	☐	☐	☐	☐	☐	☐
Secret Society	☐	☐	☐	☐	☐	☐	☐	☐	☐	☐
Strife	☐	☐	☐	☐	☐	☐	☐	☐	☐	☐
Unwed Birth	☐	☐	☐	☐	☐	☐	☐	☐	☐	☐
Violence	☐	☐	☐	☐	☐	☐	☐	☐	☐	☐
	☐	☐	☐	☐	☐	☐	☐	☐	☐	☐
	☐	☐	☐	☐	☐	☐	☐	☐	☐	☐
	☐	☐	☐	☐	☐	☐	☐	☐	☐	☐

Iniquities	S1	S2	S3	S4	S5	S6	S7	S8	S9	S10
	☐	☐	☐	☐	☐	☐	☐	☐	☐	☐
	☐	☐	☐	☐	☐	☐	☐	☐	☐	☐
	☐	☐	☐	☐	☐	☐	☐	☐	☐	☐
	☐	☐	☐	☐	☐	☐	☐	☐	☐	☐
	☐	☐	☐	☐	☐	☐	☐	☐	☐	☐
	☐	☐	☐	☐	☐	☐	☐	☐	☐	☐

Diseases/Illness	S1	S2	S3	S4	S5	S6	S7	S8	S9	S10
Alzheimer's	☐	☐	☐	☐	☐	☐	☐	☐	☐	☐
Childlessness	☐	☐	☐	☐	☐	☐	☐	☐	☐	☐
Dementia	☐	☐	☐	☐	☐	☐	☐	☐	☐	☐
Mental Illness	☐	☐	☐	☐	☐	☐	☐	☐	☐	☐
Premature Death	☐	☐	☐	☐	☐	☐	☐	☐	☐	☐
Arthritis	☐	☐	☐	☐	☐	☐	☐	☐	☐	☐
Chronic Illness	☐	☐	☐	☐	☐	☐	☐	☐	☐	☐
Heart disease	☐	☐	☐	☐	☐	☐	☐	☐	☐	☐
Miscarriage	☐	☐	☐	☐	☐	☐	☐	☐	☐	☐
Thyroid disorders	☐	☐	☐	☐	☐	☐	☐	☐	☐	☐
Cancer	☐	☐	☐	☐	☐	☐	☐	☐	☐	☐
Diabetes	☐	☐	☐	☐	☐	☐	☐	☐	☐	☐
High blood pressure	☐	☐	☐	☐	☐	☐	☐	☐	☐	☐
Multiple sclerosis	☐	☐	☐	☐	☐	☐	☐	☐	☐	☐
	☐	☐	☐	☐	☐	☐	☐	☐	☐	☐
	☐	☐	☐	☐	☐	☐	☐	☐	☐	☐
	☐	☐	☐	☐	☐	☐	☐	☐	☐	☐
	☐	☐	☐	☐	☐	☐	☐	☐	☐	☐
Total Iniquities										
Total Diseases										

Mother's Side

Iniquities	GGF	GF	F	ME	M	GM	GGM
Abortion	☐	☐	☐	☐	☐	☐	☐
Adultery	☐	☐	☐	☐	☐	☐	☐
Arrogance	☐	☐	☐	☐	☐	☐	☐
Boastful	☐	☐	☐	☐	☐	☐	☐
Child Abuse	☐	☐	☐	☐	☐	☐	☐
Criminal	☐	☐	☐	☐	☐	☐	☐
Divisive	☐	☐	☐	☐	☐	☐	☐
Envy	☐	☐	☐	☐	☐	☐	☐
Fornication	☐	☐	☐	☐	☐	☐	☐
God Hater	☐	☐	☐	☐	☐	☐	☐
Idolatry	☐	☐	☐	☐	☐	☐	☐
Lying	☐	☐	☐	☐	☐	☐	☐
Molestation	☐	☐	☐	☐	☐	☐	☐
Perfectionism	☐	☐	☐	☐	☐	☐	☐
Pride	☐	☐	☐	☐	☐	☐	☐
Rebellion	☐	☐	☐	☐	☐	☐	☐
Sexual Perversion	☐	☐	☐	☐	☐	☐	☐
Slander	☐	☐	☐	☐	☐	☐	☐
Suicide	☐	☐	☐	☐	☐	☐	☐
Unclean	☐	☐	☐	☐	☐	☐	☐
Witchcraft/Sorcery	☐	☐	☐	☐	☐	☐	☐
Abuse	☐	☐	☐	☐	☐	☐	☐
Alcoholic	☐	☐	☐	☐	☐	☐	☐
Bitterness	☐	☐	☐	☐	☐	☐	☐
Blood Shed	☐	☐	☐	☐	☐	☐	☐
Controlling	☐	☐	☐	☐	☐	☐	☐
Deceitful	☐	☐	☐	☐	☐	☐	☐
Divorce	☐	☐	☐	☐	☐	☐	☐
False Religion	☐	☐	☐	☐	☐	☐	☐
Gluttony	☐	☐	☐	☐	☐	☐	☐
Hatred	☐	☐	☐	☐	☐	☐	☐
Lack	☐	☐	☐	☐	☐	☐	☐

Iniquities	GGF	GF	F	ME	M	GM	GGM
Mammon	☐	☐	☐	☐	☐	☐	☐
Occult	☐	☐	☐	☐	☐	☐	☐
Pornography	☐	☐	☐	☐	☐	☐	☐
Prostitution	☐	☐	☐	☐	☐	☐	☐
Rejection	☐	☐	☐	☐	☐	☐	☐
Secrecy	☐	☐	☐	☐	☐	☐	☐
Stealing	☐	☐	☐	☐	☐	☐	☐
Unbelief	☐	☐	☐	☐	☐	☐	☐
Unforgiveness	☐	☐	☐	☐	☐	☐	☐
Addiction	☐	☐	☐	☐	☐	☐	☐
Anger/Rage	☐	☐	☐	☐	☐	☐	☐
Blasphemy	☐	☐	☐	☐	☐	☐	☐
Carousing	☐	☐	☐	☐	☐	☐	☐
Coveting	☐	☐	☐	☐	☐	☐	☐
Depression	☐	☐	☐	☐	☐	☐	☐
Drug Abuse	☐	☐	☐	☐	☐	☐	☐
Fearfulness	☐	☐	☐	☐	☐	☐	☐
Greed	☐	☐	☐	☐	☐	☐	☐
Hypocrite	☐	☐	☐	☐	☐	☐	☐
Lust	☐	☐	☐	☐	☐	☐	☐
Mental Illness	☐	☐	☐	☐	☐	☐	☐
Pride	☐	☐	☐	☐	☐	☐	☐
Poverty	☐	☐	☐	☐	☐	☐	☐
Quarreling	☐	☐	☐	☐	☐	☐	☐
Sexual Immorality	☐	☐	☐	☐	☐	☐	☐
Secret Society	☐	☐	☐	☐	☐	☐	☐
Strife	☐	☐	☐	☐	☐	☐	☐
Unwed Birth	☐	☐	☐	☐	☐	☐	☐
Violence	☐	☐	☐	☐	☐	☐	☐
	☐	☐	☐	☐	☐	☐	☐
	☐	☐	☐	☐	☐	☐	☐
	☐	☐	☐	☐	☐	☐	☐

Diseases/Illness	GGF	GF	F	ME	M	GM	GGM
Alzheimer's	☐	☐	☐	☐	☐	☐	☐
Childlessness	☐	☐	☐	☐	☐	☐	☐
Dementia	☐	☐	☐	☐	☐	☐	☐
Mental Illness	☐	☐	☐	☐	☐	☐	☐
Premature Death	☐	☐	☐	☐	☐	☐	☐
Arthritis	☐	☐	☐	☐	☐	☐	☐
Chronic Illness	☐	☐	☐	☐	☐	☐	☐
Heart disease	☐	☐	☐	☐	☐	☐	☐
Miscarriage	☐	☐	☐	☐	☐	☐	☐
Thyroid disorders	☐	☐	☐	☐	☐	☐	☐
Cancer	☐	☐	☐	☐	☐	☐	☐
Diabetes	☐	☐	☐	☐	☐	☐	☐
High blood pressure	☐	☐	☐	☐	☐	☐	☐
Multiple sclerosis	☐	☐	☐	☐	☐	☐	☐
	☐	☐	☐	☐	☐	☐	☐
	☐	☐	☐	☐	☐	☐	☐
Total Iniquities							
Total Diseases							

Mother's Siblings

Iniquities	S1	S2	S3	S4	S5	S6	S7	S8	S9	S10
Abortion	☐	☐	☐	☐	☐	☐	☐	☐	☐	☐
Adultery	☐	☐	☐	☐	☐	☐	☐	☐	☐	☐
Arrogance	☐	☐	☐	☐	☐	☐	☐	☐	☐	☐
Boastful	☐	☐	☐	☐	☐	☐	☐	☐	☐	☐
Child Abuse	☐	☐	☐	☐	☐	☐	☐	☐	☐	☐
Criminal	☐	☐	☐	☐	☐	☐	☐	☐	☐	☐
Divisive	☐	☐	☐	☐	☐	☐	☐	☐	☐	☐
Envy	☐	☐	☐	☐	☐	☐	☐	☐	☐	☐
Fornication	☐	☐	☐	☐	☐	☐	☐	☐	☐	☐
God Hater	☐	☐	☐	☐	☐	☐	☐	☐	☐	☐
Idolatry	☐	☐	☐	☐	☐	☐	☐	☐	☐	☐
Lying	☐	☐	☐	☐	☐	☐	☐	☐	☐	☐
Molestation	☐	☐	☐	☐	☐	☐	☐	☐	☐	☐
Perfectionism	☐	☐	☐	☐	☐	☐	☐	☐	☐	☐
Pride	☐	☐	☐	☐	☐	☐	☐	☐	☐	☐
Rebellion	☐	☐	☐	☐	☐	☐	☐	☐	☐	☐
Sexual Perversion	☐	☐	☐	☐	☐	☐	☐	☐	☐	☐
Slander	☐	☐	☐	☐	☐	☐	☐	☐	☐	☐
Suicide	☐	☐	☐	☐	☐	☐	☐	☐	☐	☐
Unclean	☐	☐	☐	☐	☐	☐	☐	☐	☐	☐
Witchcraft/Sorcery	☐	☐	☐	☐	☐	☐	☐	☐	☐	☐
Abuse	☐	☐	☐	☐	☐	☐	☐	☐	☐	☐
Alcoholic	☐	☐	☐	☐	☐	☐	☐	☐	☐	☐
Bitterness	☐	☐	☐	☐	☐	☐	☐	☐	☐	☐
Blood Shed	☐	☐	☐	☐	☐	☐	☐	☐	☐	☐
Controlling	☐	☐	☐	☐	☐	☐	☐	☐	☐	☐
Deceitful	☐	☐	☐	☐	☐	☐	☐	☐	☐	☐
Divorce	☐	☐	☐	☐	☐	☐	☐	☐	☐	☐
False Religion	☐	☐	☐	☐	☐	☐	☐	☐	☐	☐
Gluttony	☐	☐	☐	☐	☐	☐	☐	☐	☐	☐
Hatred	☐	☐	☐	☐	☐	☐	☐	☐	☐	☐
Lack	☐	☐	☐	☐	☐	☐	☐	☐	☐	☐

Iniquities	S1	S2	S3	S4	S5	S6	S7	S8	S9	S10
Mammon	☐	☐	☐	☐	☐	☐	☐	☐	☐	☐
Occult	☐	☐	☐	☐	☐	☐	☐	☐	☐	☐
Pornography	☐	☐	☐	☐	☐	☐	☐	☐	☐	☐
Prostitution	☐	☐	☐	☐	☐	☐	☐	☐	☐	☐
Rejection	☐	☐	☐	☐	☐	☐	☐	☐	☐	☐
Secrecy	☐	☐	☐	☐	☐	☐	☐	☐	☐	☐
Stealing	☐	☐	☐	☐	☐	☐	☐	☐	☐	☐
Unbelief	☐	☐	☐	☐	☐	☐	☐	☐	☐	☐
Unforgiveness	☐	☐	☐	☐	☐	☐	☐	☐	☐	☐
Addiction	☐	☐	☐	☐	☐	☐	☐	☐	☐	☐
Anger/Rage	☐	☐	☐	☐	☐	☐	☐	☐	☐	☐
Blasphemy	☐	☐	☐	☐	☐	☐	☐	☐	☐	☐
Carousing	☐	☐	☐	☐	☐	☐	☐	☐	☐	☐
Coveting	☐	☐	☐	☐	☐	☐	☐	☐	☐	☐
Depression	☐	☐	☐	☐	☐	☐	☐	☐	☐	☐
Drug Abuse	☐	☐	☐	☐	☐	☐	☐	☐	☐	☐
Fearfulness	☐	☐	☐	☐	☐	☐	☐	☐	☐	☐
Greed	☐	☐	☐	☐	☐	☐	☐	☐	☐	☐
Hypocrite	☐	☐	☐	☐	☐	☐	☐	☐	☐	☐
Lust	☐	☐	☐	☐	☐	☐	☐	☐	☐	☐
Mental Illness	☐	☐	☐	☐	☐	☐	☐	☐	☐	☐
Pride	☐	☐	☐	☐	☐	☐	☐	☐	☐	☐
Poverty	☐	☐	☐	☐	☐	☐	☐	☐	☐	☐
Quarreling	☐	☐	☐	☐	☐	☐	☐	☐	☐	☐
Sexual Immorality	☐	☐	☐	☐	☐	☐	☐	☐	☐	☐
Secret Society	☐	☐	☐	☐	☐	☐	☐	☐	☐	☐
Strife	☐	☐	☐	☐	☐	☐	☐	☐	☐	☐
Unwed Birth	☐	☐	☐	☐	☐	☐	☐	☐	☐	☐
Violence	☐	☐	☐	☐	☐	☐	☐	☐	☐	☐
	☐	☐	☐	☐	☐	☐	☐	☐	☐	☐
	☐	☐	☐	☐	☐	☐	☐	☐	☐	☐
	☐	☐	☐	☐	☐	☐	☐	☐	☐	☐

Iniquities	S1	S2	S3	S4	S5	S6	S7	S8	S9	S10
	☐	☐	☐	☐	☐	☐	☐	☐	☐	☐
	☐	☐	☐	☐	☐	☐	☐	☐	☐	☐
	☐	☐	☐	☐	☐	☐	☐	☐	☐	☐
	☐	☐	☐	☐	☐	☐	☐	☐	☐	☐
	☐	☐	☐	☐	☐	☐	☐	☐	☐	☐
	☐	☐	☐	☐	☐	☐	☐	☐	☐	☐

Diseases/Illness	S1	S2	S3	S4	S5	S6	S7	S8	S9	S10
Alzheimer's	☐	☐	☐	☐	☐	☐	☐	☐	☐	☐
Childlessness	☐	☐	☐	☐	☐	☐	☐	☐	☐	☐
Dementia	☐	☐	☐	☐	☐	☐	☐	☐	☐	☐
Mental Illness	☐	☐	☐	☐	☐	☐	☐	☐	☐	☐
Premature Death	☐	☐	☐	☐	☐	☐	☐	☐	☐	☐
Arthritis	☐	☐	☐	☐	☐	☐	☐	☐	☐	☐
Chronic Illness	☐	☐	☐	☐	☐	☐	☐	☐	☐	☐
Heart disease	☐	☐	☐	☐	☐	☐	☐	☐	☐	☐
Miscarriage	☐	☐	☐	☐	☐	☐	☐	☐	☐	☐
Thyroid disorders	☐	☐	☐	☐	☐	☐	☐	☐	☐	☐
Cancer	☐	☐	☐	☐	☐	☐	☐	☐	☐	☐
Diabetes	☐	☐	☐	☐	☐	☐	☐	☐	☐	☐
High blood pressure	☐	☐	☐	☐	☐	☐	☐	☐	☐	☐
Multiple sclerosis	☐	☐	☐	☐	☐	☐	☐	☐	☐	☐
	☐	☐	☐	☐	☐	☐	☐	☐	☐	☐
	☐	☐	☐	☐	☐	☐	☐	☐	☐	☐
	☐	☐	☐	☐	☐	☐	☐	☐	☐	☐
	☐	☐	☐	☐	☐	☐	☐	☐	☐	☐
Total Iniquities										
Total Diseases										

My Immediate Siblings

Iniquities	S1	S2	S3	S4	S5	S6	S7	S8	S9	S10
Abortion	☐	☐	☐	☐	☐	☐	☐	☐	☐	☐
Adultery	☐	☐	☐	☐	☐	☐	☐	☐	☐	☐
Arrogance	☐	☐	☐	☐	☐	☐	☐	☐	☐	☐
Boastful	☐	☐	☐	☐	☐	☐	☐	☐	☐	☐
Child Abuse	☐	☐	☐	☐	☐	☐	☐	☐	☐	☐
Criminal	☐	☐	☐	☐	☐	☐	☐	☐	☐	☐
Divisive	☐	☐	☐	☐	☐	☐	☐	☐	☐	☐
Envy	☐	☐	☐	☐	☐	☐	☐	☐	☐	☐
Fornication	☐	☐	☐	☐	☐	☐	☐	☐	☐	☐
God Hater	☐	☐	☐	☐	☐	☐	☐	☐	☐	☐
Idolatry	☐	☐	☐	☐	☐	☐	☐	☐	☐	☐
Lying	☐	☐	☐	☐	☐	☐	☐	☐	☐	☐
Molestation	☐	☐	☐	☐	☐	☐	☐	☐	☐	☐
Perfectionism	☐	☐	☐	☐	☐	☐	☐	☐	☐	☐
Pride	☐	☐	☐	☐	☐	☐	☐	☐	☐	☐
Rebellion	☐	☐	☐	☐	☐	☐	☐	☐	☐	☐
Sexual Perversion	☐	☐	☐	☐	☐	☐	☐	☐	☐	☐
Slander	☐	☐	☐	☐	☐	☐	☐	☐	☐	☐
Suicide	☐	☐	☐	☐	☐	☐	☐	☐	☐	☐
Unclean	☐	☐	☐	☐	☐	☐	☐	☐	☐	☐
Witchcraft/Sorcery	☐	☐	☐	☐	☐	☐	☐	☐	☐	☐
Abuse	☐	☐	☐	☐	☐	☐	☐	☐	☐	☐
Alcoholic	☐	☐	☐	☐	☐	☐	☐	☐	☐	☐
Bitterness	☐	☐	☐	☐	☐	☐	☐	☐	☐	☐
Blood Shed	☐	☐	☐	☐	☐	☐	☐	☐	☐	☐
Controlling	☐	☐	☐	☐	☐	☐	☐	☐	☐	☐
Deceitful	☐	☐	☐	☐	☐	☐	☐	☐	☐	☐
Divorce	☐	☐	☐	☐	☐	☐	☐	☐	☐	☐
False Religion	☐	☐	☐	☐	☐	☐	☐	☐	☐	☐
Gluttony	☐	☐	☐	☐	☐	☐	☐	☐	☐	☐
Hatred	☐	☐	☐	☐	☐	☐	☐	☐	☐	☐
Lack	☐	☐	☐	☐	☐	☐	☐	☐	☐	☐

Iniquities	S1	S2	S3	S4	S5	S6	S7	S8	S9	S10
Mammon	☐	☐	☐	☐	☐	☐	☐	☐	☐	☐
Occult	☐	☐	☐	☐	☐	☐	☐	☐	☐	☐
Pornography	☐	☐	☐	☐	☐	☐	☐	☐	☐	☐
Prostitution	☐	☐	☐	☐	☐	☐	☐	☐	☐	☐
Rejection	☐	☐	☐	☐	☐	☐	☐	☐	☐	☐
Secrecy	☐	☐	☐	☐	☐	☐	☐	☐	☐	☐
Stealing	☐	☐	☐	☐	☐	☐	☐	☐	☐	☐
Unbelief	☐	☐	☐	☐	☐	☐	☐	☐	☐	☐
Unforgiveness	☐	☐	☐	☐	☐	☐	☐	☐	☐	☐
Addiction	☐	☐	☐	☐	☐	☐	☐	☐	☐	☐
Anger/Rage	☐	☐	☐	☐	☐	☐	☐	☐	☐	☐
Blasphemy	☐	☐	☐	☐	☐	☐	☐	☐	☐	☐
Carousing	☐	☐	☐	☐	☐	☐	☐	☐	☐	☐
Coveting	☐	☐	☐	☐	☐	☐	☐	☐	☐	☐
Depression	☐	☐	☐	☐	☐	☐	☐	☐	☐	☐
Drug Abuse	☐	☐	☐	☐	☐	☐	☐	☐	☐	☐
Fearfulness	☐	☐	☐	☐	☐	☐	☐	☐	☐	☐
Greed	☐	☐	☐	☐	☐	☐	☐	☐	☐	☐
Hypocrite	☐	☐	☐	☐	☐	☐	☐	☐	☐	☐
Lust	☐	☐	☐	☐	☐	☐	☐	☐	☐	☐
Mental Illness	☐	☐	☐	☐	☐	☐	☐	☐	☐	☐
Pride	☐	☐	☐	☐	☐	☐	☐	☐	☐	☐
Poverty	☐	☐	☐	☐	☐	☐	☐	☐	☐	☐
Quarreling	☐	☐	☐	☐	☐	☐	☐	☐	☐	☐
Sexual Immorality	☐	☐	☐	☐	☐	☐	☐	☐	☐	☐
Secret Society	☐	☐	☐	☐	☐	☐	☐	☐	☐	☐
Strife	☐	☐	☐	☐	☐	☐	☐	☐	☐	☐
Unwed Birth	☐	☐	☐	☐	☐	☐	☐	☐	☐	☐
Violence	☐	☐	☐	☐	☐	☐	☐	☐	☐	☐
	☐	☐	☐	☐	☐	☐	☐	☐	☐	☐
	☐	☐	☐	☐	☐	☐	☐	☐	☐	☐
	☐	☐	☐	☐	☐	☐	☐	☐	☐	☐

Iniquities	S1	S2	S3	S4	S5	S6	S7	S8	S9	S10
	☐	☐	☐	☐	☐	☐	☐	☐	☐	☐
	☐	☐	☐	☐	☐	☐	☐	☐	☐	☐
	☐	☐	☐	☐	☐	☐	☐	☐	☐	☐
	☐	☐	☐	☐	☐	☐	☐	☐	☐	☐
	☐	☐	☐	☐	☐	☐	☐	☐	☐	☐
	☐	☐	☐	☐	☐	☐	☐	☐	☐	☐

Diseases/Illness	S1	S2	S3	S4	S5	S6	S7	S8	S9	S10
Alzheimer's	☐	☐	☐	☐	☐	☐	☐	☐	☐	☐
Childlessness	☐	☐	☐	☐	☐	☐	☐	☐	☐	☐
Dementia	☐	☐	☐	☐	☐	☐	☐	☐	☐	☐
Mental Illness	☐	☐	☐	☐	☐	☐	☐	☐	☐	☐
Premature Death	☐	☐	☐	☐	☐	☐	☐	☐	☐	☐
Arthritis	☐	☐	☐	☐	☐	☐	☐	☐	☐	☐
Chronic Illness	☐	☐	☐	☐	☐	☐	☐	☐	☐	☐
Heart disease	☐	☐	☐	☐	☐	☐	☐	☐	☐	☐
Miscarriage	☐	☐	☐	☐	☐	☐	☐	☐	☐	☐
Thyroid disorders	☐	☐	☐	☐	☐	☐	☐	☐	☐	☐
Cancer	☐	☐	☐	☐	☐	☐	☐	☐	☐	☐
Diabetes	☐	☐	☐	☐	☐	☐	☐	☐	☐	☐
High blood pressure	☐	☐	☐	☐	☐	☐	☐	☐	☐	☐
Multiple sclerosis	☐	☐	☐	☐	☐	☐	☐	☐	☐	☐
	☐	☐	☐	☐	☐	☐	☐	☐	☐	☐
	☐	☐	☐	☐	☐	☐	☐	☐	☐	☐
	☐	☐	☐	☐	☐	☐	☐	☐	☐	☐
	☐	☐	☐	☐	☐	☐	☐	☐	☐	☐
Total Iniquities										
Total Diseases										

THE BIG PICTURE

Father's Side of the Family

1. What are the generational sins of iniquity discovered?

2. How many generations were affected?

3. How did iniquity twist in your family?

4. Was their victimization associated with iniquity in your family? If so, identify it for the next generation?

5. What are the generational diseases discovered?

6. How many generations were affected?
   _____
   _____
   _____

7. What did you learn about your family?
   _____
   _____
   _____

8. Have you been caught in any of these iniquity traps that run in your family?
   _____
   _____
   _____

9. What should you watch out for?
   _____
   _____
   _____

Mother's Side of the Family

1. What are the generational sins of iniquity discovered?

   _____
   _____
   _____

2. How many generations were affected?

   _____
   _____
   _____

3. How did iniquity twist in your family?

   _____
   _____
   _____

4. Was their victimization associated with iniquity in your family? If so, identify this for the next generation?

   _____
   _____
   _____

5. What are the generational diseases discovered?

   _____
   _____
   _____

6. How many generations were affected?

   _____
   _____
   _____

7. What did you learn about your family?
   _____
   _____
   _____

8. Have you been caught in any of these iniquity traps that run in your family?
   _____
   _____
   _____

9. What should you watch out for?
   _____
   _____
   _____

Prayer to Remove Iniquity

When the enemy accuses a born-again Christian, the Heavenly Father sees the blood of Jesus. Is there any area where you are stuck? Then it is time to check your heart. Go to your Heavenly Father in prayer, ask him if there is anyone you need to forgive. Not forgiving others can keep you in bondage (Mt 18:35). Furthermore, "In your anger do not sin": Do not let the sun go down while still angry (Eph 4:26). If you find yourself angry, deal with it the same day. Forgive quickly and give the situation back to God.

Prayer to Forgive Anger.

Heavenly Father, I ask you to forgive me for holding onto anger. I release anger that I've held against_____ (*Name of Person*) for_____. (*Next pray the prayer to forgive.*)

Prayer to Forgive.

Heavenly Father I decide to forgive_____ (*Name of Person*) for_____. I forgive from my heart and release_____ (*Name of Person*) back to you. I ask that you have your way in_____ (*Name of Person*) life, according to your perfect will.

Prayers for Iniquity.

Additionally, there may be sin in your bloodline due to iniquity (Rev 12:10). Somewhere in your family line, guilt exists that has not been cleansed by the blood of Jesus. Pray the following prayer.

Prayer to Remove a Specific Iniquity.

Heavenly Father, please forgive and remove the iniquity of_____ from me and my bloodline through all generations back to Adam and Eve. Place it on the cross, never holding it against me and my bloodline again. Thank you, Father in Jesus name.

Prayer to Remove all Iniquity, Sin, and Guilt.

Heavenly Father, please forgive and completely remove all iniquity, sin, and guilt from me and my bloodline through all generations back to Adam and Eve. Place these on the cross, never allowing them to be held against me again. Thank you, Father in Jesus name.

Prayer to Remove Any Physical or Mental Illness.

Heavenly Father, I ask in the Name of Jesus that _____ *(any physical or mental illness)* which operates in my bloodline to be permanently removed and cut off by the cleansing power of the blood of Jesus Christ.

Father now I ask that you release total healing in my body from _____ *(any physical and mental illness)*. Thank you, Father in Jesus name, I receive it. Thank you for the guiltless blood of Jesus Christ that cleanses, heals, and sets me free. (**1 John 1:7, Hebrews 9:22, Leviticus 17:11,** Is 53:5; 1 Peter 2:24).

Prayer for Victims of Abuse

Father, I was a victim of abuse. What happened to me was wrong. I choose to forgive _____ of this sin against me. I renounce and break this ungodly union with _____. I ask that you cut off all physical, mental, and emotional ties from me and _____. Please remove all negative consequences of this abuse totally from my life. I thank you Jesus for your blood shed on the cross that covers, cleanses, and sets me completely free.

Prayer to Receive Family Blessings.

Father thank you for the blessings you have placed in my family bloodline. I ask that you restore all blessing to me and my family line that has been lost or stolen. Thank you, Father, I receive it in Jesus' name.

According to Joan Hunter, "when a person receives a blood transfusion or a transplant, there could be a transfer of iniquity from the bloodline of the donor. "Since generational curses are passed down through the bloodline, they can attach to a person by means of a blood transfusion, gamma globulin, human-derived insulin, or a body part transplant."[1] The prayer below will take care of it. For more specific prayers for different needs, I highly recommend Joan Hunter's book, *Healing Starts Now! Expanded Edition*.

> "Father God, I ask you to forgive and cleanse me and the donor from whom I received _____ from all sin, guilt, and iniquity all the way back to Adam. Place it all on the cross, never to be held against me and the donor again. Any generational sins from the bloodline of the donor are severed from me in the name of Jesus Thank you, Father, that you have heard and answered my prayer."[2]

The Lord told Joel that he would clean the blood of his people, and we take him at his word (Joel 3:21).

Footnotes

[1] Hunter, J., 2013. Healing Starts Now! Expanded Edition. Shippensburg: Destiny Image, Inc., p. 76.

[2] Ibid

Scripture References on Sin

For everything in the world--the lust of the flesh, the lust of the eyes, and the pride of life-- comes not from the Father but from the world (1 John 2:16 NIV). To long for the forbidden would-be lust. Eve revealed the power of lust when tempted of the devil to eat the forbidden fruit.

And when the woman saw that the tree was good for food, and that it was pleasant to the eyes, and a tree to be desired to make one wise, she took of the fruit thereof, and did eat, and gave also unto her husband with her; and he did eat. (Genesis 3:6 NIV)

Lust of the Flesh Scripture

1Therefore, since Christ suffered in his body, arm yourselves also with the same attitude, because whoever suffers in the body is done with sin. 2 That he no longer should live the rest of his time in the flesh to the lusts of men, but to the will of God. 3 For the time past of our life may suffice us to have wrought the will of the Gentiles, when we walked in lasciviousness, lusts, excess of wine, revellings, banquetings, and abominable idolatries. (1 Peter 4:2,3 NIV)

10 But chiefly them that walk after the flesh in the lust of uncleanness and despise government. Presumptuous are they, self-willed, they are not afraid to speak evil of dignities. 18 For when they speak great swelling words of vanity, they allure through the lusts of the flesh, through much wantonness, those that were clean escaped from them who live in error. (2 Peter 2:10,18 NIV)

16 These are murmurers, complainers, walking after their own lusts; and their mouth speaketh great swelling words, having men's persons in admiration because of advantage. 17 But, beloved, remember ye the words which were spoken before of the apostles of our Lord Jesus Christ; 18 How that they told you there should be mockers in the last time, who should walk after their own ungodly lusts. (Jude 1:16-18 NIV)

The acts of the flesh are obvious: sexual immorality, impurity and debauchery; idolatry and witchcraft; hatred, discord, jealousy, fits of rage, selfish ambition, dissensions, factions and envy; drunkenness, orgies, and the like. I warn you, as I did before, that those who live like this will not inherit the kingdom of God. (Galatians 5:19-21 NIV)

He went on: "What comes out of a person is what defiles them. 21For it is from within, out of a person's heart, that evil thoughts come—sexual immorality, theft, murder, 22adultery, greed, malice, deceit, lewdness, envy, slander, arrogance and folly. 23All these evils come from inside and defile a person." (Mark 7:20-23 NIV)

Lust of the Eyes

Hell and destruction are never full; so the eyes of man are never satisfied. (Proverbs 27:20 KJV)

But I say unto you, that whosoever looketh on a woman to lust after her hath committed adultery with her already in his heart. (Matthew 5:28 KJV)

Don't lust for her beauty. Don't let her coy glances seduce you. (Proverbs 6:25 NLT)

"I made a covenant with my eyes not to look lustfully at a young woman." (Job 31:1 NIV)

Pride of Life

Each one should test their own actions. Then they can take pride in themselves alone, without comparing themselves to someone else. (Galatians 6:4 NIV)

Live in harmony with one another. Do not be proud but be willing to associate with people of low position. Do not be conceited. (Romans 12:16 NIV)

Command those who are rich in this present world not to be arrogant nor to put their hope in wealth, which is so uncertain, but to put their hope in God, who richly provides us with everything for our enjoyment. (1 Timothy 6:17 NIV)

Before a downfall the heart is haughty, but humility comes before honor. (Proverbs 18:12)

20 And God spoke all these words, saying:

Ten Commandments

2 "I *am* the Lord your God, who brought you out of the land of Egypt, out of the house of [a] bondage.

3 "You shall have no other gods before Me.

4 "You shall not make for yourself a carved image—any likeness *of anything* that *is* in heaven above, or that *is* in the earth beneath, or that *is* in the water under the earth; 5 you shall not bow down to them nor [b] serve them. For I, the Lord your God, *am* a jealous God, visiting [c] the iniquity of the fathers upon the children to the third and fourth *generations* of those who hate Me, 6 but showing mercy to thousands, to those who love Me and keep My commandments.

7 "You shall not take the name of the Lord your God in vain, for the Lord will not hold *him* guiltless who takes His name in vain.

8 "Remember the Sabbath day, to keep it holy. 9 Six days you shall labor and do all your work, 10 but the seventh day *is* the Sabbath of the Lord your God. *In it* you shall do no work: you, nor your son, nor your daughter, nor your male servant, nor your female servant, nor your cattle, nor your stranger who *is* within your gates. 11 For *in* six days the Lord made the heavens and the earth, the sea, and all that *is* in them, and rested the seventh day. Therefore, the Lord blessed the Sabbath day and hallowed it.

12 "Honor your father and your mother, that your days may be long upon the land which the Lord your God is giving you.

13 "You shall not murder.

14 "You shall not commit adultery.

[15] "You shall not steal.

[16] "You shall not bear false witness against your neighbor.

[17] "You shall not covet your neighbor's house; you shall not covet your neighbor's wife, nor his male servant, nor his female servant, nor his ox, nor his donkey, nor anything that *is* your neighbor's."

www.ingramcontent.com/pod-product-compliance
Lightning Source LLC
Chambersburg PA
CBHW080551230426
43663CB00015B/2789